A Bridge to Forgiveness

A father, a daughter, and
their path to reconciliation

by

Tanya Laeger

&

Tom G. Carey

Published by Carey-Laeger
Santa Barbara, Ca.

ISBN: 9781790325597

For Karen, for her love and her commitment to finding my daughter, and for Tanya for her forgiveness.

~Tom G. Carey

For Ron, the man who brings love, life, and laughter daily into our lives and home.

~Tanya Laeger

A Bridge to Forgiveness

Acknowledgements

Nothing on these pages would have been possible without the dedicated efforts and uncanny internet research skills of my wife, Karen Sibley Carey. The encouragement of Ron Laeger inspired the collaborative writing of this book, and the acceptance, love, and support of Tanya and of my granddaughters sustained me throughout the effort.

I will forever be in debt to Cork Millner for his patience and skill in teaching me to "write from the start," and tip my hat to Robert L. McCullough for his editorial insights while putting all of what follows between covers.

~Tom G. Carey

This book is a composite of an ordinary girl who grew into an ordinary woman with the love, support and acceptance that eventually found their way into her heart. Not a day goes by that I am not eternally thankful for the joy, challenge, and perseverance my husband Ron Laeger has provided in this laboratory of love called life. My daughters, Lindsi, Kali and Misti light the world with the intelligence, grace, individuality, spunk, faith, and love now extended yet to another generation of their own making. With deep appreciation to Karen, for not letting an unrealized future go unaddressed without reaching out to this ordinary girl who now knows the love of a father she never knew.

~Tanya Laeger

A Bridge to Forgiveness

Foreword

This is the story of two lives—my father's and my own—lived apart and ultimately reunited not by happenstance or intention but by the forces of faith, compassion, and the power of forgiveness.

My father and I are collaborators here. As I tell my story, so will he tell his.

This book is neither intended as a confessional nor as an indictment of those people and events that brought us to this point. We believe that our story serves as an example that transformation is possible, emotional scars can be mended, and as a demonstration of the healing power of forgiveness.

My personal perspective is based upon my faith in God and the teachings of his son, Jesus Christ. I believe there is no greater gift than that of forgiveness, acceptance, and love.

I'll tell you all I can about my life and what has made me the woman I am, and my father will tell you what has brought him to this point in his life and in our relationship. We're all influenced—either positively or not—in some way by the people and events of our lives, and the two of us are living examples of the end products of those influences.

This is not a "tell all" story where blame is assigned, where fingers are pointed, or where guilt is judged, so neither of us are using the true names of certain of our family members simply out of respect for their personal privacy. This is not their story; it is ours.

When we come to terms with the truth of who we are, and when we fully understand who we are *meant to be*, we can then see the path ahead with clear eyes and unclouded vision.

We hope our story of self-realization and reconciliation helps to light your path, for there is no greater power in our lives and no more valuable gift we can bestow than that of forgiveness.

~ T.L.

Tom G. Carey & Tanya Laeger

Tom: Listener

'd never heard anything like it before. Her voice was strong and clear. The honesty was obvious. So was the pain.
There was no accusation.
Only raw truth.
And forgiveness.
And love.

• • • •

It was an October night in Santa Barbara. Unseasonably cool. Made cooler by my wife Karen's distant mood. Strange. Something was brewing.

We'd been married fifteen years. Karen and I met while I was an executive at a prominent construction and development firm. She was a skilled auditor at a Los Angeles real estate outfit and my company was in dire need of her skills. It was a good fit.

It didn't take long for our business to become personal. She was everything a man could wish for: beautiful, brilliant, and—in spite of personal medical challenges that she overcame with energy and determination—we fell deeply in love. The fact that I was still in my third marriage at the time was certainly a problem, but nothing that some artful lies on my part couldn't handle. Once the truth of our affair and the revelation of an earlier marriage was known by my wife, divorce quickly followed and then Karen and I tied the knot. We've been life partners and business partners ever since.

Our marriage has been unlike any of my prior three. No secrets. Total honesty. Open books. I'd been a liar and a cheat through three marriages and I wasn't going to go through that again. I'm committed to Karen and I'm not going to fall back into old patterns.

No more lies. Nothing but truth, communication, honesty. We talk about everything with total transparency and open hearts. It's my newfound obsession.

That's why that October night was so different. The chill in the air had nothing to do with the weather.

Lying together in bed, she finally turned to me and came up on one elbow. Eye contact.

"What do you think about having three grandchildren?" she said.

I could feel my face flush. She thought I had kept something, some part of the past, some part of the truth from her. That I had done what I had been so good at through my three earlier marriages, lied by omission.

"I didn't know I had grandchildren or I would've told you." The truth.

Karen knew of my lifelong guilt and shame for having essentially abandoned my first child—a little girl—when she was just three years old. For many years Karen had heard me try to justify leaving the girl with my first wife and never seeing her again. And now justifications were evaporating.

"Do you want to know about your daughter and your grandchildren?" she asked.

It was the obvious question. Not necessarily the one I was prepared to hear, so I dodged it. "You know I tried reaching out a long time ago, and it didn't work out. I'm not really comfortable about intruding on her life. Not after all this time." Weak, but my "not being comfortable" had served as a pretty good justification for avoiding things more than once before.

Karen sat up now. Her voice cracked. "Well, you should listen to the testimonial I downloaded."

That got my attention. I didn't know what she was talking about or why she was so choked up. Emotional.

My own father had recently passed away. I immediately realized Karen had been using her formidable online research skills to research my twisted family tree. "Does this have something to do with my father's obituary?" I asked.

She reached over and touched my arm. The chill in the air warmed, but I sensed this all had something to do with her never having a child of her own. We'd spent more than a decade together. Traveling together. Working on business deals together. Living the good life together. From the time we started dating, I'd told Karen I was done being a parent. I'd failed miserably at that job. It was agreed: there would be no more children.

That agreement didn't survive more than a few years into the marriage. Maybe she changed her mind because of the good times we'd had with her nieces and nephews. Or maybe it was just the ticking of her biological clock growing more resonant.

The conversations became more difficult, but I held my ground. My argument was clear, if not particularly romantic: I was simply too old to start another family. I'd had a vasectomy. I was already carrying the guilt of having three grown kids with whom I had no relationship. I wasn't the poster boy for fatherhood.

So when she touched my arm that night, there was definitely something behind it. Karen knew how I'd buried the pain of not having any connection with my daughter or my two sons. Now she had a way of making me face those failures. A way of forcing me to deal with the pain. A way of ripping away any justification for avoiding the truth. "You need to hear this," she said.

I knew this was about my daughter. I wasn't at all eager to deal with the pain of my long-buried guilt over things in the distant past. But as Karen pushed the "play" button on her iPad, I listened, never expecting that what I was about to hear would change things forever.

I didn't even recognize the soft voice that drew me in...

"My husband Ron asked me to talk about my experience because he knows I have had a long and winding road in my "journey of forgiveness." For me, it hadn't been easy, and my forgiveness has not been a one time and forget it kind of deal.

I sought a way to forgive authentically, without dismissing the realities of what has taken place in my life. What Jesus said on the

3

cross became my mantra: 'Father forgive them, for they don't know what they do.'

I began to apply that to my own life, to use it as I deal with the reality of my relationship with my biological dad, for he had no idea that abandoning and rejecting his daughter would have lingering effects of insecurity and my internal feelings of not being wanted or loved."

Those words, and the voice speaking them, forced me to face an elusive, painful truth and to take a step forward to begin my own journey.

4

Tanya: Testimonial

The book "Doorway to Discipleship" talks about symbolically inviting Jesus into the rooms of our spiritual house. We allow Jesus to turn on the lights, arrange furniture in rooms where the family gathers and enjoys the company of one another.

Attempting to live a life of faith and devotion—my husband is a pastor, after all—I believed I had allowed Jesus into every room of my spiritual house. But, like the 1970s TV detective "Columbo," there always seemed to be "just one more thing..."

As we raised children and lived our very busy lives, every once in a while something would happen that triggered within me a deep anxiety and an overriding fear. I wasn't sure what it was, but it was clearly the Lord letting me know I had some unpacked baggage hidden in the dark recesses of the attic of my spiritual house.

That baggage had always been safely tucked away in the darkness and dust of my attic, only to be visited when the uninvited guests of anxiety and fear would drop in, quite unannounced.

It was time. Jesus lovingly let me know that He and I needed to climb the stairs of my spiritual house and visit my attic. This would be the night He would turn on the attic light so we could examine my baggage together."

· · · ·

My husband never intended to be a pastor, but he is one. I was just sixteen when I sat with my girlfriends in the bleachers at a Centralia Tigers High School baseball game and became immediately transfixed with the second baseman, Number 16. I never missed a game that season.

As inexperienced and tentative as I was, I somehow mustered the courage to approach Number 16 and asked him to go with me to the

"Tolo," the only dance of the school year when the girls are supposed to ask the boys.

He smiled down at me and agreed to be my date. In my mind, God had answered a prayer I was too afraid to ask.

Ron was easy to love: tall, charismatic, charming, and filled with a sense of pure adventure. Three months later, I was wearing his Promise Ring and finally knew the feeling of being wanted, of being loved. That Promise Ring held great meaning for both of us, representing an emotional commitment between kindred spirits. We saw in each other a soul companion, someone we could share our lives with and whom we could depend on.

During Christmas break of my senior year of high school, as we sat in front of a Nativity Scene on the shores of Capital Lake in Olympia, Washington, Ron proposed with these words: "I can't promise you we'll ever be rich, but if you marry me, your life will never be boring."

A promise made, and a promise kept. Even at eighteen, Ron was a natural leader, fascinated by politics, a supporter of America's military, and a believer in traditional American family values. He spoke to me of his ambition to become a U.S. Senator by the age of fifty, and immediately got busy working at the local fire station, earned his Emergency Medical Technician certification at eighteen, and was known locally as a real go-getter who exuded confidence and knew his way around in the world.

I was more than smitten; I was a fan, a loyal supporter, and completely dependent on his love.

His family were dedicated church-goers while I had never even been exposed to the tradition of Sunday services or the protocols they entail. When Ron asked me to attend church with him, it was an eye-opener. People were decked out in their Sunday finest, singing songs I'd never heard, and everyone passing the wooden offertory dish up and down the rows of pews. I became mesmerized at the booming sound of the pastor's voice from the pulpit as he spoke about the teaching of Jesus and the meaning of Easter.

Of course, I was seriously perplexed when the congregation began singing a hymn about "Blood of the Lamb" and I noticed a bathtub sitting squarely in the middle of the altar. I had no idea what to expect, fearing a slaughter of a lamb in that bathtub was in our future, which

6

was a pretty clear indication of my religious background up to that point.

Within a couple of months, though, I came to understand the figurative references in the lyrics of some hymns, and that the bathtub was used for baptisms, one of the many church traditions I was unfamiliar with, but would eventually grow to understand and even participate in. Much of this was explained to me by my very patient and loving fiancé, while the message of a loving God delivered from the pulpit in that booming pastor's voice stirred something deep within me.

If God was real, I truly wanted to know Him so I could ask the questions to which I so desperately needed some answers.

Up to that point, I'd spent much of my life in an emotional void, a dark space where abandonment, rejection, and abuse at the hands of those who were supposed to be my fathers undermined each of my days. Now, at the age of eighteen, just one month after my high school graduation, I had my young knight in shining armor, a man who would love me, a man who—either by accident, design, or through God's love—would ultimately help me shine a light into that dark void.

Brilliant young men with ambition to match their abilities can be difficult to distract from their goals. Ron was working full time at his family's business, taking a full course load as a college freshman, volunteering at the local Chamber of Commerce, working in regional political campaigns, helping to build our first house, and serving as the youngest Fire Commissioner in the State of Washington. All were admirable endeavors, none of which had much to do with getting a young marriage off to a healthy start.

I was anxious to leave my parents' home, and on July 16, 1982, just one month after graduating high school, Number 16 and I were married. When Ron came to ask my stepfather for my hand in marriage, my dad got up from the living room couch, left the room and didn't return. A week later, he took Ron to lunch and finally gave his approval. Such were the power plays I would soon leave behind when Ron and I would have a family of our own.

Within three months of our wedding, however, my own fears and insecurities, born of my quiet childhood of abandonment, abuse, and anxiety began to weigh heavily. Ron had promised our lives together would not be boring, and he kept that promise to its fullest; our lives were hectic, rushed, distracted...and growing apart.

I was soon wondering if any man would ever truly love me, if my fears and insecurities would ever subside. I got down on my knees and prayed. I hoped that if no one else would, maybe God would love me.

I simply couldn't face those suitcases in my attic on my own.

Tom: Hoboken, 1950

The fear and the deception began in first grade.

The problems were fundamental.

Knowing my right hand from my left. "Raise your right hand and state your full name and address," Mrs. James told the class. My name is called and my left hand flies up. "Don't you know your left hand from your right?" she said, setting the tone for the next ten years of my formal education.

Learning the letters of the alphabet. An impossible challenge. While I struggle to distinguish between letters, my classmates are soon forming words, reading. I don't know what's wrong as my brain flickers on and off; moments of clarity followed by moments of total confusion.

But I'm clever. I quickly devise "work arounds" to overcome what is clearly my personal failing. I learn to use silence, to visualize, to mimic, to manipulate, to obfuscate, to avoid the truth.

Mrs. James starts with the first row. Each student will stand and read aloud to the class. "Thomas, please stand and read page six" strikes me with terror. I do my best, reading with uncertainty, stumbling over words I can't recognize. Her patience wears thin. "Take a seat in the back of the class" is the sentence for my crime.

The brutal comments of my first grade classmates become the mantra of my daily life. My choices are limited: lash out angrily or make myself invisible.

I vanish. I become emotionally, socially, academically absent. They can no longer hurt me because I no longer care.

Gloria. My loving mother who tried so hard, who sat with me at the kitchen table spelling out the words on my weekly spelling tests. My loving mother who patiently taught me to sound words out, who couldn't hide her disappointment when I failed each spelling test.

Thomas. He gave me his name. For the next sixteen years, he punished me for using it.

1209 Willow Avenue. I sit on the fifth floor fire escape looking at the street far below, mesmerized by the 5:00 p.m. rush of people far below. Ants returning to their nests.

Then I see him, parking his car a full block away. I have breathing room for ten minutes, the time it will take him to walk back to our tenement and climb the stairs to our cramped apartment.

A thud. He pushes open the entry door to the building as though it is in his way. I rush to my chair at the formica-topped table. I know my place and dare not be out of it.

He washes his hands, sits at the table with no eye contact, no words other than "What's for dinner?" Gloria dutifully sets dinner plates down. "Let's eat" is his response.

Dinner conversation is limited to his recitation of his hatred for all of humanity. No racial epithet goes unspoken. The venom in his voice singes my ears. Gloria tries to change the topic or ask a question and she's shouted down for challenging his authority. I sit rigidly, ordered into silence.

His plate is empty and he leaves for the living room. The sound of the radio tells me I can now leave the table. In cold weather there was no place to go except into the living room where he was listening to "You Can't Take It With You." In the warmer months the fire escape landing beckoned and I climbed out the window to my perch where I could be safe, out of harm's way, listening to the music of the Hoboken nights.

Thomas George Carey Sr. bullied his way through life. He was a threatening, insecure man with a sixth-grade education who used his six-foot-two bulk to intimidate all over whom his shadow fell.

The day I understood the depth of his internal rage, I was eight years old. I'd made the mistake of crossing our Hoboken street without permission and then compounded that crime by coming home late for dinner. My mother, upset and worried, told my father about my transgression when he walked in the door

10

that night. He took that as a personal challenge to his authority, and immediately threw me onto the bed, unbuckled his inch-and-a-half wide belt and went to work.

My mother, suddenly regretting she'd mentioned my tardiness and never dreaming a savage beating would follow, could do nothing to stop him. She screamed at him as he ate dinner that night, but he never answered her.

I awakened the next morning battered, with welts on my back, arms, and legs. Walking was difficult. I stayed home from school that day and my mother promised me he would never hit me again. That promise was kept, but life with my father became a test of endurance, living with daily threats of violence and angry silence.

Something died inside of me. I would live in that house for another eight years. Each of those days was marked by fear. Each of those days marked another step as I withdrew further and further into myself.

Will I ever forgive my father?

Maybe. Someday.

But not yet.

Tanya: Port Jervis, 1964

I've always taken a secret pride—feeling a bit special, really—at having been born in New York, not that Port Jervis is what people usually think about when the Empire State comes to mind.

My parents met when Tom was stationed in Port Hueneme, California's quintessential Navy town fifty miles north of Los Angeles, and Marilyn was living with her grandparents and working behind the counter at the Port Hueneme Naval Base movie theater. One night, a tall blonde sailor approached and asked about the price of a bag of popcorn.

"What's your name?" my future mother asked my future father. They both quickly forgot about the popcorn.

The shy, handsome sailor and the red-haired California beauty each filled the needs of the other. Just weeks later, they stood at the altar of the Ventura Community Church where country singer Johnny Cash was reputedly a congregant and where my parents were invited by the pastor to enunciate their wedding vows. Neither my mother's nor my father's parents attended the ceremony; they wouldn't meet their respective daughter- or son-in-law until months after the ink was dry on their marriage certificate.

Tom and Marilyn—now husband and wife—were both eighteen years old. Because my mother was still in school and a minor, my father—just eighteen himself, but a *bona fide* member of the United States Navy—would be required to sign her final report cards prior to her high school graduation.

As the daughter of a "screamer," my mother's early family life had been turbulent and emotionally destructive, so escaping into the arms of a tall, handsome, charismatic sailor was a perfectly reasonable path to her self- anointed maturity and the security of young love, however fragile that might prove to be.

Tom was promptly reassigned to a duty station in Norfolk, Virginia, where he was stationed aboard a ship bound for the Mediterranean.

When she discovered she was pregnant, my mother went to live with Tom's parents in Pennsylvania which his mother Gloria insisted was a great place to have a baby.

It was an early February morning with deep snow on the ground when Tom rushed my mother to the Port Jervis hospital over the Delaware Bridge and across the New York state line. Thirty-six hours of hard labor later, at the hands of a doctor with an aversion to Caesarian deliveries—in spite of my full-breech orientation to the world—I entered the world, battered and bruised. That difficult journey through the birth canal may have foreshadowed the challenges I would face later in life and may lie at the foundation of my lifelong yearning for emotional security and safety.

Once I was properly swaddled and in my mother's arms, we crossed the Delaware Bridge and once again returned to my grandparents' home in Pennsylvania's easternmost municipality, the town of Matamoros. My mother's independent and adventurous spirit made leaving the warm shores of California and her family an easy choice. She was in love. And love won the day. But by the time my mother unpacked and had me tucked into my crib, Tom was on his way to Norfolk and his berth on the USS Mount McKinley.

Two weeks later he would be a working sailor on board one of America's historically significant force command ships, sailing off in pursuit of a young man's freedom and adventure. He would return to his young family still carrying the paternal curse of his own childhood.

• • • •

"After I was born, my father pushed my mother and me down a flight of stairs. At that point, Mom finally decided to leave him. One day I was living with Mommy and Daddy, the next day I didn't have a daddy any more. There would be no birthday cards, no calls, no contact of any kind.

"Along with packing my favorite life-sized doll with the pink floppy hat in the suitcase, I also packed with me that day the shoes of abandonment in the suitcase of my mind."

14

Tom: The Recruit

N aval Induction Center, 39 Whitehall Street. New York City, 1961. This is where I would shed my sixteen years of childhood.

I fell into line with 40 other young men. We stepped forward, raised our right hands, and repeated the words shouted at us:

"I, Thomas Carey, do solemnly swear that I will support and defend the Constitution of the United States against all enemies, foreign and domestic, that I will bear true faith and allegiance to the same, and that I will obey the orders of the President of the United States and the orders of the officers appointed over me, according to regulations and the Uniform Code of Military Justice, so help me God."

The shouting voice ricocheted off the concrete walls of the induction center: *"Congratulations. You're now sailors in the U.S. Navy."*

My heart pounded. I was finally free. I was no longer the son of Thomas G. Carey, Sr.

I was Number 32 today, a sailor, a man. Unspoken went my rage at a childhood of fear. I locked away the scars and the heartache. I ignored my yearning for acceptance, for love.

I follow Number 31 as we board the olive-drab bus. In my hands are scant medical records and my DD 4-1 Form. In my chest, pride, hope, and anxiety begin to brew.

The Great Lakes, Michigan U.S. Naval Training Center is nothing like the streets of Hoboken. Heads are shaved, stiff new uniforms are issued, and I fall under the command of Training Instructor Chief Petty Officer Johnson.

Chief Johnson is a task master. He expects adherence to the precepts of *The Bluejacket's Manual*, the bible of the U.S. Navy, packed with 600 pages of rules, regulations, protocols, and ethics. Chapter 4 defines honorable ways of behavior. Good rules for those in the military and for those who are not.

I now have a father figure I can respect. Chief Johnson shows no favoritism. He's strict but not abusive. He cares about us, wants us to succeed.

He also wants us to write letters home. Upon hearing that, my throat tightens. The alphabet. Words. Elusive, difficult to decipher in a mind constantly dodging contact with them, always preferring manipulative tactics of avoidance and deception.

Why write letters when I can just use the phone? And so I did, avoiding the written word, avoiding the embarrassment of anyone ever seeing the depths of my illiteracy.

Following boot camp, I was transferred to Naval Air Station Cecil Field, Jacksonville, Florida. It was the farthest I'd ever been from Hoboken. Far from my father's anger, endless disapproval, and constant threats of violence. It was freedom, freedom to find love on my own terms.

I was seventeen years old in starched Navy whites in an environment that contrasted starkly with New Jersey or Michigan. By comparison, Jacksonville was sultry, tropical. Off the base, men wore Hawaiian shirts and women wore short skirts.

The climate did little to fill my overriding need for approval, for acceptance, for love. That would be a job for Linda, a true southern beauty with the personality of pure Florida sunshine. True safety for a boy with a heart broken by his childhood.

Linda accepted my proposal of marriage, so I called home early in the day, knowing my father would not pick up the phone.

16

I eagerly told my mother that her son was now engaged to marry the woman he loved.

Silence. And then, my mother's voice in all its clarity and finality: "You're too young to get married, Tom. You need to take some time with this."

I listened with quiet indifference. I was in the Navy. I knew what I was doing. "I know what I want and I know what I'm doing." The conversation was over. I needed love and I needed it now.

Linda and I were engaged. But she would never get the chance to give me the love I needed.

Tom G. Carey & Tanya Laeger

Tanya: Dream

My father received his discharge from the Navy in 1966, shortly after his return from his second cruise aboard the USS Mount McKinley.

I was 18 months old. My mother had been living with Tom's parents in Pennsylvania, but she'd never forgotten the feeling of the the warm California sun on her face and the Pacific Ocean at her feet.

Since his return to civilian life, my father's voice had grown loud. He and Mom would argue over many things: money, living with in-laws, suspected infidelities.

My mother suggested they return to the place where they had fallen in love, where they had married, where their life together had been happy. Life would be better. Tom would settle down, find work and discover the joys of a loving family.

Looking for something—himself—and hoping to escape the pain of his own childhood, Tom agreed. With a car filled with expectations, a toddler, and all their worldly possessions, Tom and Marilyn set out on a seven day cross-country trip that would take them back to Port Hueneme.

It was going to be the California Dream.

Tom G. Carey & Tanya Laeger

Tom: Safe

The year was 1963. I was assigned to Seabee Base Drafting Illustrator School, Port Hueneme, California. Not exactly hard duty for my second duty station, considering the fact that America's involvement in Southeast Asia was making news.

I was 3,000 miles away from Linda, who was still in Jacksonville. I was 3,000 miles away from anyone who would fill my nights with affection, acceptance, love. I was 3,000 miles away from a salve for my loneliness.

As an 18-year-old on the loose in Southern California, it was only a matter of weeks before that would change. After a day of classes, a balmy night of boredom led me to the base movie theater. Sean Connery in *From Russia with Love* would kill a couple of hours.

Marilyn stood behind the concession counter. A young redhead with a smile as bright as any movie screen. I looked at the selection of candy, making a very careful, prolonged decision.

"What's your name?" Her husky voice killed my appetite for sweets and welcomed me into her heart. In the years since, I realize that at that moment I had translated those words into "I'll make you safe."

Marilyn's offer of safety clouded my vision, rationalized any infidelity, and allowed me to justify leaving Linda where she suddenly was: forgotten. Marilyn's affections eradicated my loneliness, my wanting, my insecurity. For the next month, I saw Sean Connery for a few minutes every night.

I've often wondered what Marilyn saw in me, a shy, skinny kid from Hoboken. My vulnerability and fragile nature may have been a lure. Maybe it was my obvious infatuation with her youthful independence and adventuresome spirit. She was only

21

seventeen, living with her sister, and as eager as I was for security. Like me, she was looking for someone to love who would love her in return.

I was just beginning to understand my abilities with pencil and pen. Days spent studying drafting and illustration were teaching me how to quickly cover mistakes with darker strokes, to obscure my fledgling skills with layers of false technique. I was beginning to use a similar trick in my life: to layer over problems with another pattern, to change colors and cast false shadows. I had no awareness of fine art, but later I would appreciate the techniques of the Flemish masters and their ability to trick the eye with light and shadows. I would pile on layer upon layer of lies to the canvas of my life. I was practicing the art of falsehood to create the perception of truth where there was none.

In what had become a mechanism of childhood survival— lying by omission—I never told Marilyn about Linda. She would never know I was already engaged to another. I would never tell her. I would paint the dark colors of deception over all that would follow.

During my last phone call with Linda, I asked her to return her engagement ring. I justified our breakup easily. "I don't love you. You don't make me feel safe." The stunning degree of my selfish narcissism of fifty years ago rings in my ears even now.

I called home for the second time to tell my mother I was once again engaged. No words of caution or reason could dissuade me. Marilyn was just 17 and I was an impulsive 18. We married in a small community church, close to where we first saw each other, under the watchful eye of Sean Connery.

We had each escaped our oppressive childhoods. We had found each other.

We were safe.

Tanya: Norfolk

My mother had become a Navy wife. Follow the fleet. Adventure awaits.

Tom's shore duty in California came to an end when he was reassigned to Naval Station Norfolk, Virginia. My young father would become part of the United States Fleet Forces Command with operations throughout the Atlantic and the Mediterranean.

His transfer was immediate. It didn't matter that on the day Tom received his orders to report to Norfolk. Mom had announced she was pregnant, but orders were orders.

The young parents-to-be left California bound for the frigid Atlantic coast, armed only with their youth, vitality, and vague hopes for the future.

In Norfolk, the young couple lived in married housing quarters on the Navy base until he received sailing orders. He was to board the USS Mount McKinley and prepare to ship out, bound for a three-month Mediterranean deployment.

Two weeks before weighing anchor, Tom drove my pregnant mother north to his parents' home in Matamoros, Pennsylvania. The consensus was that it would be the best place to bring a baby into the world.

My seventeen-year-old pregnant mother would sleep in a house my father could never live in himself.

Tom G. Carey & Tanya Laeger

Tom: Wonder

In Norfolk, we lived in base housing married quarters. My adjustment to marriage, to making peace with the fact that I was responsible for this teenage girl, was abrupt.

Three years of comfortable shore duty came to an equally abrupt end and, in 1964, I shipped out for the Mediterranean.

Even then, as a self-centered manipulator, I worried that I was leaving my pregnant young wife in Pennsylvania, in the same house with my father, the one man in the world I feared most. I trusted that she would be protected by my mother, a woman I viewed in the fantasy-warm hues of endless maternal love.

The voyage across the Atlantic and into the Mediterranean was a spectacular adventure for the boy from Hoboken. Shore leave in Italy—a country with a unique cultural heritage and the birthplace of my grandparents—was both an education and an inspiration. I would return many times.

The trip was punctuated by Marilyn's due date. It was the middle of February when the Navy's paternity leave provided me with air transport back to Norfolk.

Once I set foot on U.S. soil, I drove north to Pennsylvania to be there the night Tanya was born.

Fresh snow blanketed Matamoros, covering roads and houses in glistening white. Only passing snow plows broke the night silence as I drove Marilyn across the Delaware Bridge to the hospital in Port Jervis. February 19, 1964 was a day of joy as Tanya entered our world at full volume.

Marilyn and I shared the wonder of our daughter.

I made promises. I would never allow the sort of anger and fear I had endured in my father's home to become a part of our lives.

The images of Tanya's first years remain indelible, drawn with warm shades of dusty pastels in my mind even as I write this.

Tiny hands wrapped around my finger.
Bright laughter, enjoying the world around her.
A Cheerio finds her mouth as others litter the floor.
Giggles.
Tickles.
Heart-melting hugs.
It was a happiness beyond happiness.
Feelings I could not endure.
The memories of those short years linger, but their pastel images would be erased by the dark shades of anger, fear, and lies.

Tanya: Return

Tom was honorably discharged from the Navy on his 21st birthday. With four years of dutiful service to his country behind him, he drove straight from Norfolk to Matamoros, scooped us up and off we went back to my "hometown" of Port Jervis, easternmost burg of The Empire State.

I was talking and walking, a true New Yorker by the time I was two.

That was the year of loud voices.

Fear, confusion, insecurity.

This would be my "triple crown" that I would wear well into adulthood.

Tom had skills he'd learned in the Navy, but he felt constrained by the limitations of a small town that was being passed over by the public prosperity and unlimited horizons of The Sixties.

His anger, frustration, and guilt surfaced as his father's once had. My world was filled with my father's hostility toward my mother, the world, himself. He carried his father with him.

My mother suggested a change: return to California where the days are warmer, where economic opportunities are the news of the day. Any change would be an improvement, a promise of peace, a cessation of hostilities.

Our little family of three packed all our worldly belongings into the car and headed west, ostensibly so my mother could be closer to her family. The truth was in her fervent hope that California would calm the anger always simmering inside my father. He would find work, fulfill his desire to go back to school, and we'd live happily ever after.

Days, weeks, months of tranquility were eclipsed by the trauma of daily shouting matches between my parents. I believe each of us is born with certain strengths and specific sensitivities. With each argument, my little heart shriveled, never feeling safe or secure, always wondering if this was how families were supposed to be.

I was clearly a sensitive little girl, aware of all that was going on around me, recording each of the good times and each of the frightening times on my toddler's internal hard drive. The human heart is fragile, yet capable of great strength.

But all I had was my triple crown of fear, confusion, and insecurity.

My strength was yet to come, and it would be years before I would find it.

.

Tom: Demon

Everything was packed into my black Dodge convertible. We looked back and waved to my mother, Gloria. She had just kissed Tanya in a tearful goodbye.

My father had made himself scarce. He was not to be seen.

Grandma watched us go from the porch. Her warmth, the light that kept me safe from my father, dims and flickers. The old Victorian house disappeared as we looked back through the dusty Dodge's rear window. Life as we had known it was now just a memory, a thing of the past.

I did a good job, I knew, of hiding my fears. I cleverly disguised the Demon who was my constant companion. He was a beast who could reveal himself at any time to terrify my young wife and daughter. It was the Demon's fault, never mine.

We headed west on Route 66, pushed forward by our naïve hopes and expectations. Things would be better in California, just seven days and eight states away.

At the start, hemlock and mountain laurel lingered in the air. Marilyn played games and told Tanya stories of beaches and of the ocean that awaited us. Her stories told of a fresh start for us. We would be the loving parents of a cherished little girl.

"What are you thinking?" Marilyn asked. Tanya was asleep, swaddled in blankets on the back seat.

"I want to go back to school." I kept my eyes on the road.

Marilyn snapped the road map open, putting the icing on her cold silence.

The Navy had taught me the value of an education. I knew that my future depended on getting one, and the G.I. Bill could make that possible.

Marilyn had other reasons for returning to California which had nothing to do with my being away from her and Tanya. She wanted to rebuild our relationship and see me get a job and settle down.

Hot desert aromas, the anticipation of Oxnard's fragrant strawberry fields, and Marilyn's story-telling did nothing to distract me from what I sensed deeply: my feeling of abandonment.

I had left home for the second time. And I had done so without resolving any of my issues with my father. I hated him and I wanted him to know why. But I was in the grip of paralyzing fear at the thought of ever confronting him with even a molecule of truth.

I thought back to the first time I had returned home. To a new baby, a loving wife, a doting grandmother.

Then, I had moved Marilyn and Tanya out of that house, away with me, simply to avoid my emotions, my anger, my resentment toward my father.

As I drove westward with the sun in my eyes, gripping the Dodge's steering wheel, I knew that no matter how many miles I put between myself and Thomas G. Carey, Sr., I could not escape my fury, my rage, and my deep insecurity. Aside from my inherited dyslexia, I had a far more challenging disease, a sickness passed to me by my father: unbridled anger.

Our trip took seven days. On the last day, we crossed the California state line at Needles. We navigated through increasingly heavy traffic across Southern California and found our way to U.S. 101. Cool, salty air greeted us as we pulled into Port Hueneme. "We're here!" began as a whisper and was soon a joyful shout. Baby Tanya awakened in the town where she would celebrate her second birthday.

I was 22 now, a Navy veteran eager to get the education that was the key to financial security for my young family. Marilyn and I shared the dream of a fresh start.

I had served in the military, learned much, discovered rudimentary talents, and become a man. I had married a lovely young woman and fathered a beautiful little girl.

None of that mattered.

The Demon was there in California, waiting for me.

Tanya: Voices

I was nearly three years old.

We lived close to the ocean.

I could always smell it in the mornings when the breeze blew cold, damp air onto the shore, across the beach, across the Ventura Freeway, and onto the agricultural fields of El Rio.

In the afternoons, the wind would shift, blowing heat and dust from fields across the warm sands of Oxnard's beaches. My mother would take me to the beach on those days and we would wiggle our toes in the sand and watch the glistening waves.

My father was not at home to play with me during the day. He had a job now, and was going to school. He was a busy man, and I had my mother to play with and to take care of me.

The nights were different.

My teenage mother and her young husband would talk about things beyond my understanding. All I knew was that their voices would become louder the more they talked.

I wished they would just stop talking, because the talking became shouting, yelling, frightening.

We were supposed to be a family. We were in California now, far away from everyone back east, where things were so cold, where things were so frightening.

I was supposed to be happy because Daddy and Mommy were supposed to be happy.

But at night, their voices weren't happy. Not at all.

I sat up in bed. The night air was filled with a brewing storm. I leaned against the wood bed frame, wearing my favorite pink-footie pajamas and holding close my large stuffed doll with an oversized pink hat.

I saw the shadows of Daddy and Mommy moving in the light at the bottom of the bedroom door. Their voices thundered through the keyhole and rolled under the door, amplified by the wood floor.

My body tensed, my stomach ached, and my eyes burned with tears. What was happening? Why were they yelling at each other? What if something happens? Where would I go?

Terror of the unknown rose in the back of my throat.

I could feel the weight of my triple crown. Confusion stoked my fear, and fear fed my insecurity.

I was waiting to be happy, to be loved.

Instead, I was about to go from having a Mommy and a Daddy to not having a Daddy at all.

Tom: Deceit

It didn't take long for the reality of our new life in California to become apparent.

We left New York and drove 3,000 miles in search of things that remained elusive.

Financial security would not come quickly. My salary as a fledgling technical illustrator put food on the table and paid the rent, but provided very little more. We were living in a small bungalow in El Rio, a dusty farming community on the wrong side of the freeway. On some mornings you could smell the ocean five miles away. On others you could smell the pesticides from the broccoli and strawberry fields. El Rio was nobody's concept of the California lifestyle.

Unlike Marilyn, I wasn't that concerned with where we lived or how. I was focused on other things.

I had been discharged from the Navy just as the Vietnam conflict was becoming a critical national issue. As a service veteran, I was entitled to benefits that gave me a second chance at an education, and I intended to take advantage of them.

The transition from the military to college life was not without its challenges. After four years in the Navy, I was at least four years older than the other freshman students at Ventura Junior College.

I suppose Marilyn could sense my awkwardness and insecurity, so she introduced me to her younger cousin, Sandy, who was already in her Sophomore year at Ventura JC.

Sandy would show me the ropes and help me get registered and acclimated to the campus. Sandy was younger than Marilyn, another true California girl with Nordic good looks and a blonde pixie-cut hairstyle.

We met in the new students' registration line. Once I had my classes, she showed me around the sprawling campus. She asked about my life in the Navy and I regaled her with stories about my Mediterranean cruise and my time in Italy. She seemed thoroughly intrigued by what I had to say.

Once classes started, Sandy and I would meet on campus and talk about a wide range of things, all of them feeding my need for attention, for acceptance.

None of our conversations ever touched upon the fact that I was married to her cousin and was the father of a three-year-old daughter. That was not an oversight by either of us. It was simply me performing my old trick of deception through manipulation, of avoiding the truth by simply omitting it from the dialogue. The deception was mine to make, and I was the one whom I most eagerly deceived.

My insecurities seemed to vanish with her flirtatious demonstration of interest in all things "Tom." I was soon completely enamored, and for all the wrong reasons.

It didn't take long for flirtations to become intimate interludes. I was a married man, but my ego didn't care. I knew the difference between right and wrong, between loyalty and infidelity, but I didn't care.

While my young classmates were acting out the rebellious innocence of their youth by wearing long hair and bellbottoms and marching in the streets to protest America's involvement in Vietnam, I was busy going to class and betraying my wife.

At home, seeds of suspicion began to take root. I justified my long absences throughout the day with a work and school schedule that kept me away from Marilyn and Tanya all day and most nights. Marilyn knew I was determined to do well academically, as I was focused on earning my Associate of Arts degree and then transferring to a four-year college to study architecture.

But even the most artful liar—and I was just that—can never maintain a subterfuge when he depends upon his co-conspirators to do the same. Marilyn began asking pointed questions about the time I spent at school, comparing my class schedule to Sandy's. Our nightly arguments over money became shouting matches laced with accusations of infidelity.

I—the boy who had learned the magic of "work arounds" to disguise my severe dyslexia, the man who had never read Chapter 4 of *the Blulejacket's* Manual outlining a Navy man's moral responsibilities, but who had written the rule book on deception, distraction, and duplicity—lied with a perfectly straight face. My root-level insecurities were disguised by my own rampant self-deception. Was it the thrill of getting away with something forbidden? Was it an irresistibly attractive girl feeding my fragile ego? Was it a self-loathing that demanded risk-taking until all I cared for was destroyed? Would I only be truly happy with a life reduced to ashes?

Those are questions I never dared to ask. After all, I was the smarter one in the marriage. I knew that any explanations I used as a defense to Marilyn's point-by-point indictment would be impossible for her to refute.

The lies were the colors on the evolving portrait of my life. Dark shades of blue and grey. They obscured all the other colors of my canvas, made the truth invisible. I used those colors with the conviction of a masterful painter, in bold strokes. The lies were what I lived for, and I was good at them.

Until Sandy called.

Tanya: Falling

They had argued before.

The shouting had been frightening before.

This was different.

My mother picked up the phone. It was her cousin, Sandy.

What she heard on the other end turned her face white. She put the phone down and turned to my father, screaming louder than I thought was possible. "I'm leaving! I'm taking Tanya!"

My father denied the affair. He had explanations. His sense of outrage at such a preposterous accusation was vehement, strident, aggressive. So sure of himself.

Until my mother informed him that her cousin Sandy had not only just now reported having had a protracted affair with him, but that Sandy was now pregnant with his child.

The final straw was now on the camel's back, and the camel's back was broken. There was no going back.

My mother picked me up and walked out the door, heading for the outside stairs leading to the apartment's parking lot.

Tom followed us, both of them shouting loudly, my mother using words I'd never heard her speak before, Tom passionately pursuing us. The red-headed mother with a flaring temper of her own confronting an angry, defensive man about to be left alone was not a good combination.

And then my father, out of control and enraged at the thought of losing us, angrily reached out and pushed my mother off the stairway landing. She fell down the entire flight of stairs with me in her arms.

I was on the ground at the bottom of the stairs, stunned. My mother, battered and bruised, was beside me in a crumpled heap. I don't remember crying, only thinking for the first time that the world was an unsafe place where bad things can happen.

I was only three years old, but I was right. Bad things can happen.

Tom: Haunted

The affair with Sandy was easy to deny.

It was just so preposterous, wasn't it?

We had serious financial difficulties, to be sure. We were living on the second floor of a dreary apartment building in Oxnard. The Dodge convertible that brought us across the country to our new life had been repossessed. There was no denying the fact that these were stressful times.

I had plenty of excuses to explain why I was so distant, why I seemed constantly distracted, why I failed to display any affection to my wife.

I was working hard at my job, dedicated to my studies at school. Besides, Sandy was Marilyn's cousin, wasn't she? Yes, of course she was attractive, yes I thought she was cute, but how did that make me guilty of anything?

Marilyn didn't believe a word of it. Her verbal attack was as loud and threatening as any of the battleship guns I'd heard in the Navy.

An attack requires a defense, a reply in kind. My fear and insecurities demanded that I respond, and I did.

I followed her out of the apartment, denying her absurd allegations of infidelity just as aggressively as she made them. When we reached the top of the landing, I reached out to grab her. She pulled away, slipped, and fell down the stairs, landing on the ground with Tanya in her arms. It happened in an instant, but it felt like it took forever.

Was that actually the case? Or have I blocked the truth out of my mind, lied to myself constantly over the years? Have I used the dark hues of my self-deception to paint over the terrifying image of my beautiful wife lying on the ground with my child in her arms?

The truth is beyond my knowing, always in the eye of the beholder. Tanya's memory of that day is vivid; mine is obscured by the fear, passion, guilt, and anger I felt at that moment and have felt every moment since.

Maybe Tanya's memory has been affected by what she has heard ("Your father pushed us down the stairs in an angry rage."). Maybe mine has been colored in a wash of the dark pigments of the past in an effort to accept my own actions.

Which is true? I cannot say.

The images of that day haunt me. My child in her mother's arms at the bottom of the stairs is a picture seared on the canvas of my mind.

That canvas holds multiple layers of brush strokes. Obscured beneath them is a portrait I cannot bear to see. The paint is many years old now, some of it brittle and hard. When I peel it away, I see immaturity, insecurity, anger, deceit, and a lifetime of bad choices.

The portrait is not an attractive one. It depicts an angry young man unaware of who he is and what he is becoming. His eyes reflect his ignorance of the destructive life and painful relationships that lie ahead.

His image haunts me to this day.

Behind his empty eyes is the Demon.

Tanya: Gone

I was the the only child in our family trio. The happily-ever-after family where I was loved, where my mother loved my father and my father responded with his undying affection, devotion, strength, and loyalty. We played together, we loved together, we lived together and we protected each other from all the bad things out there in the real world.

And then the real world raised its ferociously destructive head and, just as reality often does, destroyed it all.

The morning after the yelling and the accusations and the violence, I knew my father had not slept in my parents' bedroom. He and my mother had not hugged. They had not kissed each other goodnight. The sun came in through my window, but it was quiet. No voices, no getting-ready-to-go-to work banter.

Silence.

And then Mommy came into my room. With her came my fear, wearing a cloak of dread.

"Time to wake up," Marilyn said with a catch in a proud monotone. No smile. Minutes later, she had me dressed. "Your father is coming to see you. Wait for him outside."

I stood in the front yard, wearing the clothes Mommy had picked out for me: baby-blue dress, shiny white-patent shoes with the straps one buckle hole too tight. My white-blonde pigtails were tied with a blue satin ribbon. The grass at the bottom of the stairs where we had fallen the day before was desiccated, withered from lack of water and the seasonal sun. Vivid details, as though watching an accident unfold in slow motion.

I could see the specter of Mommy and me still lying there at the bottom of those stairs. Stunned, terrified. There was a whisper in my ear, telling me my world was coming to an end, that I was about to be pushed off a precipice.

My father's car pulled into the driveway. He left the engine running as he walked toward me in his white t-shirt, a pack of cigarettes rolled up one sleeve, Navy style. He was my father, and with the deafening roar of impending disaster swirling around my head, I was both glad to see him and afraid of him. Something deep inside wanted things to be safe again, like they were before the fall down the stairs. I wanted and needed protection from the storms of life. Maybe it was all a mistake. Maybe he was back home to hug me, to love me. Maybe hope would vanquish reality.

He moved toward me. Slow steps, his head down, his eyes avoiding mine. He leaned over, put his hands on my shoulders. "Tanya, I have to leave you for a while." I held my breath. This had to be a mistake that he would surely correct with his next words. "Remember, I love you."

A kiss on the top of my head, right between my pigtails, one of the last kisses he would ever give me. Maybe it was the way he held me, or the tone in his voice. Or maybe a cloud blocked out the sun and a shadow swept over my face. He walked back to his car as tears rolled down my cheeks.

And then he was gone. There would be a few Saturday afternoon visits, but it wasn't long before my father would never again gaze into the eyes that matched his own. He would never speak words of affirmation or love for me to hear. There would be no birthday cards, no Christmas gifts, no taking my arm to walk me down the aisle on my wedding day.

There would be nothing to indicate his awareness that in his youth he had passed his DNA to a frail little girl who believed he was everything in life.

I was three years old.

He was my universe.

And now he was gone.

Tom: Approved

I didn't cry.

I didn't explain.

I inhaled her sweet aroma as I kissed the top of the head of the little girl I loved beyond her knowing.

There was nothing more to say, so I said nothing more, and I walked away. Always holding it in, always concealing my feelings, protecting myself from any pain, from any truth.

As I put the car in gear, I saw her blue eyes, red face, and quivering chin in the rear view mirror.

I had to go. And I was gone.

I lied to myself. I told myself it would all be okay. All I had to do was put another layer of paint over this picture. Justification was such a handy tool.

Marilyn moved back in with her family. I certainly couldn't afford our two bedroom apartment, so I walked out on our lease. I paid the price in bad credit and a worse landlord reference.

I saw Tanya on weekends. What does a 22-year-old father with no money to spare do with a three year-old daughter on a Saturday? Many things, I'm sure, but all I remember are long afternoons in the park. Swings. Slides.

But narcissism and insecurity quickly became a veil that blinded me to everything around me. Perhaps that's why I now have so few memories of those days in the park. I was fully consumed with Tom Carey, Jr. and what he needed.

Who would love me now? I was alone and unloved. Where would I find an emotional connection? Where would I find someone to ask "What's your name?" and reassure this child he was loved?

Marilyn filed for divorce. Reconciliation was not going to be in her picture.

The routine of my job served as an anchor. I had someplace to go, a place where I was expected, where my work ethic was valued. I had been 14 when my father demanded I pay my share of the family rent. "You need to know how hard it is to make a buck." That left an imprint on me as vivid as the bruise his stinging back-hand put on my face.

I showed up every day for work, but I needed a roof over my head. I had been working as a part-time bartender at The Rudder Room in Oxnard. The owner offered me a room in his "pool house" in exchange for wages. Not exactly a Doris Day-Rock Hudson version of a pool house, this was nothing more than a room attached to a garage, completely out of sight of any swimming pool. No kitchen, with a sofa bed next to the whirring pool pumps, chlorine fumes, and leaking filters. It was tolerable for a Navy veteran, but not acceptable for a three-year-old overnight guest.

I avoided spending much time in the "pool house." To blunt the loneliness of my new single life, The Rudder Room became an escape. I would work behind the bar until closing time or sit quietly nursing a few beers before we turned off the lights. Sleeping on a pool table was better than inhaling chlorine and mold back in my room.

At the bar, I would watch others dance to scratchy jukebox music on the linoleum dance floor. Always in fear of a put-down or rejection, I wasn't exactly outgoing or much of a conversationalist. My inner child could be safe in his silence.

Late one night, egged on by a co-worker, I took a dare and asked a tall exotic woman to dance. "What's your name?" rang in my ears. She was interested in me, ready to accept me.

It was the one thing I needed, and so we danced.

The Demon approved.

Tanya: Rebounding

I was three, and Daddy was gone.

I had already lived in five different places, three on the East Coast and two on the West. Some people would have enjoyed the always unpredictable lifestyle of nomadic change.

I'm not one of those people. Even today, as an adult, my security and joy comes from routine, from the familiarity of home and family.

Things had indeed changed once again. No more arguments, no more shouting, no more hugs, no more being held in the arms of my Daddy, Tom.

We moved into a smaller apartment, where I would go to bed in my pink onesies, clinging to my favorite stuffed doll with the big pink floppy hat. I would whisper "Good night, Daddy" to a father who was no longer there, living in our home like daddy's are supposed to do.

My mother's bitterness over his infidelity meant that there would be no pictures or reminders of him in our home, for they had been promptly disposed of. The betrayal she had suffered and the man responsible for it deserved nothing less than total eradication from our lives.

All these years later, I can only imagine the loneliness and desperation my mother felt as soon as she and Tom separated. She was a single mother before working women were commonplace. She was still young, still beautiful. But when looks and youth are a woman's primary commodities, time is not on her side.

Marilyn quickly filed for divorce from my father. Before the ink was dry, she was married again. I remember nothing about him or the circumstances of that abbreviated union, because within months that marriage was annulled.

But my young mother would not look back, only forward, for that would be where she could find a man to trust, a man who would care for us and protect us from anything that might hurt us.

We left Oxnard for the warmer shores of Coronado, almost 200 miles to the south, across the bay from San Diego. Coronado Island is a busy resort area and the home of a U.S. Naval Air Station as well as the U.S. Navy Seal Team. The presence of the military meant that housing in the area was in high demand.

When my mother found an apartment she could afford, she found herself in competition with another man eager to rent the unit, but with a four-year old in pigtails at her side, my mother's rental application was chosen over his.

Within that first month, undoubtedly distracted by me, she absent-mindedly set a grocery bag on the electric stove's hot burner and started a small fire. Billowing smoke alerted the new neighbor who quickly came to the rescue and extinguished the fire. That new neighbor was the same man who had applied for our apartment.

Dennis Winters was an incredible physical specimen, a true warrior and the living embodiment of what it meant to be a Navy SEAL. When he put the fire out on our stove, Dennis was stationed at Coronado's Naval Amphibious Base in the last months of his SEAL training course at the Naval Special Warfare Training Center.

In the late 1960s, Basic Underwater Demolition/SEAL training was something of a covert enterprise, a response to President Kennedy's determination to build a fighting force capable of dealing with any military threat potentially posed by Russia's premier Nikita Khrushchev. Any man accepted for SEAL training was acknowledged to be extraordinary in all the ways a man could be.

Dennis Winters was strong, handsome, and wore his uniform with true command presence. Mom was smitten.

She dragged me along to watch Dennis train on a beach in front of the Hotel del Coronado, where his group practiced parachute jumps complete with sulfurous yellow smoke contrails. It was an exciting thing to see as we sat on the warm sand overlooking the pristine Pacific Ocean.

It wasn't long after Dennis earned his SEAL Trident that he and my mother would be married on that same sand. The bride and groom each wore shorts and flip-flops in true laid-back Southern California style. The ceremony was attended by Dennis' SEAL teammates, a Justice of the Peace...and wide-eyed me. There were no family members of either the groom or the bride.

It didn't matter. I had a new Daddy.

Tom G. Carey & Tanya Laeger

Tom: Dancer

Her name was Nancy.

We danced. We held each other. She smiled and laughed at all the right times.

I felt like a man. Not like a frightened boy in hiding.

We talked late into the night, the young ex-sailor and the older, beautiful Port Hueneme High School French teacher.

I learned that her father had died when she was young and she had grown up with her brother, sister, and mother. She had somehow become a nurturer, caring for her siblings without a father in the house.

She was completely open with me. She had strength and confidence where I had so little. Everything she told me was the truth.

I shared my recent past with her, told her I was recently divorced and the father of a little girl. No mention of the affair with Marilyn's cousin, of course. A simple lie of omission, what I was always good at.

Our shared passion for one another became a true romance. It was love, and I needed it like a drowning man needs air.

When she announced "You should know I don't want children," inside I felt a sense of relief. Not only could I avoid the complications of another child and a deepening of the guilt I already felt over being away from Tanya, but I could have this woman all to myself. She would love only me.

Not long after we met, I left my "pool house" and accepted Nancy's offer to crash on the sofa in the Oxnard beach house she shared with three roommates. Four women and me. Her roommates weren't too thrilled, but I felt like John Ritter in the TV show *Three's Company*. My insatiable insecurity was nicely camouflaged by a young man's apparent ego. When I moved from the sofa into Nancy's bedroom, the order of things in the female-dominated house was suddenly askew.

Tension ruled the day. Friendships became strained and resentment festered until the day Nancy and I announced we were were getting married.

Nancy got a younger student-husband, her roommates got their house back, and I found the shelter and protection I desperately wanted.

I was accepted into the architecture program at Cal Poly in San Luis Obispo. Nearly 150 miles away from Oxnard and Port Hueneme. We decided to move to Santa Barbara, a midpoint. Nancy would commute to her work in Oxnard. I would drive north to complete my degree.

By then, Marilyn had taken Tanya to Coronado and married another Navy man. A SEAL, no less. At least my baby girl would be safe. Visits with Tanya would become more difficult. Coronado was far away. I was busy.

Graduation, another move to Camarillo, the opening and closing of my first architectural office, a short stint as a male model in Los Angeles, and finally a job as an architectural associate with the University of California at Santa Barbara. It all followed in perfect, lock-step sequence.

I had refined my "work-arounds" to the point of establishing myself as a knowing, competent professional. My insecurities were mine to hide, and I hid them well. I had accomplished much, all while keeping my true self hidden away.

Appearances were everything. I had no use for any truth unless it served to protect the weak, frightened boy I refused to recognize. I had a sophisticated palette of dark colors now. I could paint over each of my shortcomings, one by one. No one would ever see the duplicitous, unfaithful liar lurking inside. I was good at my craft, a master of subterfuge.

Once I'd earned my architect's license, I abandoned the security of working as a designer for the University of California at Santa Barbara to pursue my dream of becoming an Architect/Developer. I would become a mover-and-a-shaker, a man of prestige, power, wealth. I became obsessed by my own ambitions and would do whatever it took to achieve them.

I soon learned there were real social and economic barriers to overcome. There are certain standards, high expectations of intellectual fluency, creative demands, and ethical maturity. I knew that the world of high finance and serious real estate development would never accept a dyslexic wracked with a child's fears and insecurities. It was obvious that living on Nancy's high school teacher's salary and my fledgling architects wages wouldn't be enough.

I determined to hide my reading disability from the world. I would disguise my anger and my pain. I knew I was a competent architect. But would that be enough? Could I maintain an image of emotional strength, professional loyalty, and personal honesty?

I had all the externals in place now.

In Nancy, I had a lovely, attractive, intelligent wife who had supported me throughout my schooling and stood by me while I moved up the professional ladder. We lived in a beautiful home. My need for approval and acceptance had been fulfilled. Nancy tolerated my selfishness and my workaholic drive. We both managed to ignore a certain emptiness creeping into our relationship, so the relationship managed to hold together.

I had perfected a lifetime's worth of "work arounds" and manipulative skills. I knew I had talent as an illustrator and designer. I understood the value of a nice smile and a firm handshake. I knew the rules of the game. I knew I could play with the big boys and win.

But how?

I would seize every opportunity.

I would present a false face of confidence.

I would protect the frightened boy inside.

I would manipulate.

I would be unfaithful to my wife.

I would feed my ego whatever it needed.

I would let the Demon run wild.

Tom G. Carey & Tanya Laeger

Tanya: Wondering

I was in heaven.

Mommy was happy with her new husband and I was happy with the fluffy orange shag carpet of our new apartment and being just steps away from the warm beach sands of Coronado Island.

Living on the other side of the island from the spectacular Hotel del Coronado resort, in a small town blessed by the climate of a semi-tropical paradise was this four year-old's dream. Playing on pristine, uncrowded beaches, splashing in crystal clear bay water, going on bike rides with my mother and falling asleep at her friends' beach parties became the rhythm of my life.

I was finally safe, finally secure, finally happy.

Just a short walk to the beach from our Orange Street apartment, I could watch the construction of the San Diego-Coronado Bridge, two miles of concrete and steel, stretching across the bay 200 feet above the water. It was a miracle, watching hundreds of men and machines as they slowly connected every post and beam high above the bay, slowly edging ever closer to our little island.

Even as a four year-old, I realized the power of bridges to connect us, to overcome formerly insurmountable obstacles, to bring people who had long been separated together again. I was five when the Coronado Bridge was finally completed in August of 1969. It would always inspire me to build the bridges I hoped would connect the pieces of my life.

Because my new stepfather was a SEAL, he would often disappear for weeks or months on end. Such is the *modus operandi* of the U.S. Navy's elite fighting force. Dennis Winters' deployments were always of a seriously clandestine nature of indeterminate length, so my mother busied herself with shopping trips across the U.S.-Mexican border into Tijuana where we would buy trinkets and crafts with which she would decorate our small upstairs apartment just yards from the waves of the Pacific.

When Dennis—by now I was encouraged to call him "Daddy"—was home on leave, it was decided that it was time for his newly-created family to visit his family of origin. My mother and I had never met any of his family members, and so we headed north to Oregon to do just that.

Mom and I—decked out in new outfits bought just for the trip—both looked forward to meeting my new grandparents, certain that the long drive up Interstate 5 would be well worth the fun of connecting with a new family of cousins, aunts, and uncles.

Coming from the balmy shores of Coronado, the first thing that caught my eye as we drove through the mountain roads of Oregon was the rain. When it wasn't actively raining, it was actively drizzling. The sun was nowhere to be seen.

At my mother's insistence—she was nervous about making the best possible impression on her new in-laws—we stopped at a roadside gas station to "freshen up" before driving the last couple of miles to the home of Dennis' parents.

I was busy looking at the long stretch of running river that paralleled the two lane road when we finally turned onto an unpaved gravel driveway. We bounced along for what felt like forever and finally came to a stop in the muddy driveway of a decrepit single-wide mobile home that hadn't been mobile since the day it had been dragged into place just off the main highway. Behind it stood a wooden shack where my new grandpa made his prized moonshine whiskey.

Mom was silent as we alighted from the car. I stepped onto the muddy ground in my new white patent-leather shoes. As we walked past the home's "dishwasher"—a crude table stacked high with filthy dishes and cooking pans that we came to understand would be hosed down every couple of days for re-use—I stared wide-eyed at the chickens who seemed to have the run of the place.

We stepped up onto the porch and Grandpa Winters stepped outside to greet us. I couldn't really see his eyes behind thick, dirty eyeglasses. Perfunctory greetings were exchanged between Dennis and his father, at which point Mom and I were presented to the wrinkled woman sitting on the threadbare porch couch. "This is your new granddaughter," my mother said by way of introduction.

"She's not my *real* granddaughter," said Wrinkles. And thus began another relationship for me that, like others I had already experienced,

54

was forged in a cold cauldron of rejection. The reality was clear: I was not included as part of this new family.

"Into the suitcase of my mind, I neatly folded my new little dress of rejection and being unwanted in my new little family."

I'm certain some sort of meal was served, but what I remember most about that night was my grandfather asking me If I wanted to watch a movie. Of course I did. Anything to escape the reality of where I was and whom I was with.

I was never so relieved to see "Snow White and the Seven Dwarfs" appear on the television screen. Within a minute, however, what I thought would be a familiar cartoon was revealed as "Snow White Does the Seven Dwarfs," complete with animated depictions of grossly pornographic sex acts.

My mother promptly whisked me off into the back bedroom while my grandparents laughed at the evening's video entertainment. But the bedroom was equally disturbing. Filth was everywhere. I didn't understand where I was or why I was there. All I knew is that I was sickened and terrified. On the dresser in front of me, in a small glass jar of cloudy water sat a set of stained dentures. Some children may have been fascinated by such a sight, but my sensitive, tentative, fearful nature nearly caused me to vomit.

From outside what felt like a horror chamber, I could hear the sounds of Snow White being violated by dwarfs and all I could do was sit there on that filthy brown and green bedspread and quietly sob. I was terrified. This was not a safe place, not at all.

Into my mind popped the sounds of a TV show I had heard, the theme from "The Munsters":

> "They're creepy and they're kooky,
> Mysterious and spooky,
> They're altogether ooky,
> My step-dad's family."

The next day we left to visit my new cousins. They lived in the woods with no bathroom, no electricity, and apparently no soap. The kids were older than me, but they were skinny with stomachs that stuck out. My new uncle was missing his front teeth and smelled like nothing I had ever smelled before. We soon discovered there was no running

55

water or indoor bathroom facilities in the shanty they called home. It was my first exposure to the concept of an outhouse. They were nice to me, like you would be nice to a visiting Martian, curious about who I was and where I came from.

It was a family trip that made me long for home. Reflecting upon that traumatic childhood experience, I'm sure that trip is, to a certain degree, the reason I'm not attracted to new adventures, new places, new people. Home meant safety. My own bed with the same blanket and my overstuffed doll with the pink floppy hat. Safe.

During the long drive home, listening to my new stepfather talk about his accomplishments since leaving home to join the Navy. There seemed to be an undertone of embarrassment at having to expose his new family to what he had worked so hard to leave behind. After that first trip, I don't remember ever visiting there again.

I wondered what my real father would think of the "new family" I'd just met. Were all new families like that? Was my real father getting a new family too?

Finally back home in Coronado, tucked safely back into my familiar room with my familiar bed, with my familiar pillow and my familiar warm blankets and wearing my own pajamas now, I was relieved to be far away from my stepfather's strange family. I hugged my overstuffed doll with the pink floppy hat and whispered a good night to my real father, Tom.

I looked up at the ceiling and wondered why he had pushed my mother down those stairs.

I wondered where he was.

I wondered why he didn't come to see me.

I wondered if he thought of me.

I wondered if he ever whispered good night to me, the little girl he left behind.

Tom: Ambition

N ancy understood my burning desire to do more. I had worked very hard, studied design in Italy, subjected myself to the doldrums of working as a draftsman and then as an associate architect on my way to becoming fully licensed and accredited by the American Institute of Architecture.

Even as a fully-accredited American Institute of Architects professional, it's an unpredictable career that could easily become mundane. The world is full of professional architects who sit at drafting tables calculating minimum square footages for compliance with governmental regulations.

I did not want that kind of life, working under someone else, drawing plans for their designs, with my income limited by the whim of others.

I wanted more.

I wanted the brass ring that comes with being a heavy-hitting architect-developer.

Nancy, secure in the fact that her teaching salary gave us an income base—though not nearly enough for my grasping instincts—gave me free rein to abandon my own fledgling architecture business. I gave up my office lease and took my name off the door. Now all I had to do was find a place where I could learn the ropes of real estate development.

The business community in Santa Barbara is closely knit and insular. Connections are made through personal introductions. To develop a recognizable profile, it takes relationships with people who are acquainted with each other. To break into the inner circle of "connected people" is a matter of being around the right people. I made it my objective to do just that. By attending the right arts functions, contributing to the right community charities, and joining the right business groups, I became a person of interest.

That interest lead to an invitation to join the city's preeminent design and development firm. It was a managerial position, overseeing various projects for the company. I was in the cat bird seat, learning the business from the inside out. I was on the way up, rubbing shoulders with the most powerful people in the city.

And then I heard the words that have always quickened my pulse, drawn me in like a moth to flame: "What's your name?"

Trudi was a young architect in the firm. Sprightly, bright, energetic, with a fast, incisive mind. We shared the same birthday, April 23rd. We had both earned our architectural degrees at California Polytechnic Institute. We had both studied in Florence, Italy.

We had so much in common.

Except that I was married and she was not.

The Demon didn't care.

Where Nancy was older than I was, I was 14 years older than Trudi. Youth, energy, intelligence, professional affinity only added to the appeal of a woman whose own father just happened to be successful real estate developer himself. To become his son-in-law would be an indisputable family connection. I would be on a par with those "connected people" whose favor I was constantly seeking. I'd be one of them now. I was convinced that with Trudi at my side, I'd be getting access to something akin to a private club. I would be one of them, one of the big boys, untouchable.

Fully convinced by all I'd seen, and having learned that success in the world of local real estate development required certain appearances, I realized that being married to a teacher at Port Heuneme High School simply wasn't in my best interests.

The words I spoke to the woman who had protected me, nurtured me, loved me for 12 years were coarse, to the point, and devastating. Nancy deserved none of it, but I was already somewhere else at that point. My ego and narcissism were unchained, eager to be fed by a younger woman with a father who had connections.

My last conversation with Nancy was difficult. Bitter and final. I made my usual manipulative, evasive apologies, but she saw through them. Her pain was too great to believe my usual "work arounds" and dodges. The pain I caused her that night could never be healed, and it never has been to this day. When I walked out on my marriage to Nancy, I was destroying another human being.

And the Demon didn't care.

It was time to leave that past behind, time to paint over my canvas with bright new colors no one could possibly see through.

Tom G. Carey & Tanya Laeger

Tanya: Dreams

I was forgotten, left behind by a father, the memory of whom was quickly fading from my young mind.

My life was now with my new Daddy and my mother.

As soon as Dennis mustered out of the Navy, he was offered the customary cloak-and-dagger work with the CIA. But his dream was to move to the Pacific Northwest, where hunting, fishing, and the rural lifestyle suited him best, and where he would be closer to his family, a family that truly terrified me.

Mom initially resisted the move, reminding him that I was about to enter school, that the Southern California climate was what she preferred, that she had friends there, and that she was not really comfortable living a "backwoods" lifestyle.

Her words fell on deaf ears. Dennis Winters was not a man accustomed to having his wishes denied. If Oregon was too "backwoods" for my mother, California was to "posh" for his tastes. A move to Washington State—in a process akin to true "Goldilocks" decision-making—would be "just right" for us.

After carefully packing my oversized stuffed doll with the pink floppy hat, now significantly tattered and worn after being held so tightly night after night as I wondered about my "real Daddy" and where he could be, I sat in the back seat of the car gazing out the rear window as we crossed the Coronado Bridge for the last time. The bay waters below shimmered as though bidding me farewell. Before long the home I had known and loved disappeared from sight.

If feelings of safety and security come from knowing your place in the world, what little I had evaporated in the bright sunlight on that day.

· · · ·

I wasn't quite yet five years old, so I wasn't consulted on the final decision about where we would finally settle down as a family. The compromise to move to Washington agreed to by my mother lead us to Centralia, Washington, halfway between the Oregon border and Seattle. It's a small, former logging town straddling Interstate 5, now surviving on tourism drawn to its expanding collection of outlet stores, and a state away from my new stepfather's scary family.

We moved into a rental house that allowed me to continue my childhood fascination with bridge construction, as a viaduct was under construction practically in our front yard. As a quiet, reserved little girl, watching the cranes and heavy equipment at work as they cast a shadow over our house became my primary entertainment. The aroma wafting over us from Harold's Hamburger Drive-Thru just yards away added to the ambiance and was the staple of our family meals that year, in spite of the fact that my stepfather collected unemployment benefits for several months after our move.

As an only child enduring the upheavals of constant relocation, my insecurities only festered, and when I was enrolled at elementary school, I was completely unprepared for the onslaught of 25 rambunctious, aggressively socialized classmates. Learning in an environment where 5-year-old boys were allowed to express themselves in the most obnoxious ways didn't make it easy for me to get through each day.

Because my mother had always soothed my anxious nature by telling me stories and reading to me, I had an affinity for words and decoding their meanings, and on the very first day of First Grade, I was promoted to the "Readers Circle." My pride and sense of accomplishment was short-lived. I moved to my new seat to join the handful of other fluent readers, but as I sat down one of the boys pulled the chair out from under me and I fell backward onto the floor with a painful and startling thump.

The hot flush of humiliation far beyond mere embarrassment must have been obvious, but I managed to regain my feet and take my seat without even acknowledging the laughter that filled the room or the taunting fingers that were pointed at me. I simply pretended that nothing hurt, that I barely noticed what had just happened. The reality was that I held my chin up until it was practically pointing at the ceiling, letting my tears pool on my bottom eyelids rather than allow

62

them to cascade down my cheeks. The ensuing stomach cramps, painful as they were, were unseen by anyone, for I was becoming quite the expert at suppressing my true reactions and stuffing my feelings into that suitcase of my repressed emotions, where I fully intended to leave them, forgotten.

But feelings stuffed into a suitcase and hidden away in an emotional attic don't go away. The attic is always there even if the door is locked, and no matter how deep into the shadows the suitcase is stored, the contents of that suitcase don't evaporate. If anything, they marinate and multiply, feeding on their own pain.

After yet another move, by the time I was in the Second Grade at the R.E. Bennett School, I discovered other feelings, other embarrassments, other sources of pain that would haunt me forever.

I became expert at showing the world a stoic, guarded countenance, bereft of any emotional expression. Regardless of what turmoil I might feel inside, I appeared amiable, compliant, ready to please. But when I was chosen over the other girls in the class to appear in the local newspaper's Valentine's Day issue kissing a second grade boy, I balked. I couldn't bring myself to kiss that obnoxious, chubby boy who had been part of my humiliation on that first day of First Grade. I simply declined the offer to appear on the front page of the paper kissing this boy on the cheek.

That week, when the newspaper was published, there he was...being kissed on *both* cheeks by my classmates Penny and her twin sister Paige. My feelings of jealousy were a surprise to me. It was a curious new emotion with which I was unfamiliar, and which I was unable to reconcile. I didn't want to be in that silly paper kissing that obnoxious boy, but I didn't want anyone else doing it either. Emotions would continue to perplex and confuse me, often undefined and not to be trusted.

It was just after we moved once again, away from the viaduct construction's noise and dust, when I began having terrifying recurring nightmares. The new house was small, two stories, with my upstairs bedroom facing the street in front.

The details of my repeated nightmares are consistent and clear: *I'm standing at my bedroom window, looking out onto the street. A white van with solid rear doors—no windows—pulls up in front of the house, and two men climb out of it and walk up to our house. They sneak into the house, by which point I'm fully rigid with horrific fear. I hear them climbing up the stairs as they come to my room to take me away. In my sleep, I actually hear them coming for me, and I'm paralyzed, unable to scream or call out to alert my mother and my stepfather, Dennis. The two men enter my room and take me away. I'm transported to a dark cave, chiseled out of cold, wet rock. Above me, the cave is a dome. Naked men, women, and children are shackled to the stone walls all the way up to the top of the dome. And then*—I would awaken in a cold sweat, shivering with fear.

I was seven years old when I first had this nightmare, and I was afraid to tell anyone about it for fear I would be thought strange, that a little girl shouldn't be having such dreams. So instead of telling my mother or anyone else, I internalized it, never understanding what could possibly make me see such things in my slumber, and quietly packed it into that suitcase of repressed anxieties and fears so that it would be forever safe, hidden away from the world in the secret attic of my mind.

It is said that dreams have underlying meaning; something the subconscious works on while in deepest sleep. I don't know what these repeated nightmares may have meant. Were they caused by my feelings of isolation and alienation in a cruel world with no one to rescue me? Whatever it was, all I wanted was to go to sleep and dream of pleasant thoughts, like all other seven-year-olds.

I couldn't identify the source of my anxieties, but whatever gave me those nightmares would pale by comparison to the nightmare I would eventually face while wide awake.

Tom: Unsatisfied

I filed for divorce from Nancy quickly. I couldn't let Trudi slip through my fingers. She represented an opportunity. As her husband, I would be the son-in-law of a successful developer. I would be following in his footsteps. I would be closer to the brass ring. My ambitions and my ego would be satisfied.

When Trudi told her Jewish parents she had accepted my proposal of marriage, their response was predictable. She was given their list of strong objections. I was not Jewish. I was too old for her. I was recently divorced. I was not worthy of her.

All true.

But Trudi was nothing if not strong-willed, articulate, and intelligent. She needed none of those qualities in refuting her parents' objections; she simply declared her love for me and was going to marry me. My late great-great grandmother, being Jewish, was my slender tie to Judaism and my ticket to the wedding featuring me as the groom. I was the only representative of the Carey clan at the wedding, but that was enough.

We exchanged traditional vows to love, honor, and obey. Trudi was now my wife.

All I had to do was keep the truth from her.

I was a master of subterfuge. Lying came to me as naturally as combing my hair.

I couldn't tell Trudi about my first failed marriage. I couldn't tell her I had a child, a girl of grade school age.

So I didn't.

I justified it, of course. It was a simple omission of something that would have no effect on our life together because it had stopped having an effect upon mine. What worked for me—a father who had walked out on his child and surrendered her to a new stepfather—would surely work for everyone.

Trudi and I were a genuine power couple. We both left the development firm where we had first met to form The Carey Group. We specialized in land acquisition and property development. We built everything from apartments and condos to mixed-use commercial to industrial and warehouse space, and collected fees for our services as architects, contractors, and real estate brokers.

With introductions provided by my new father-in-law—a man who drove a Rolls Royce, lived in a fine home, and flew in his own King Air Turbo Jet—lenders lined up to provide us with financing and became our partners during a decade that saw property values climb with no apparent end in sight.

But, visible or not, there is always an end somewhere beyond the horizon.

In 1982, President Reagan passed the Garn-St. Germain Act, which gave savings and loan institutions the freedom to make questionable loans with virtually no cash to back them up. Four years later, thousands of banks and savings and loans went bankrupt. Suddenly, it was a world of spread sheets and computerized financial projections. All that mattered were the numbers. Handshake deals were a thing of the past.

So was my father-in-law. He went broke fast and hard. Cars, planes, furniture, homes, jewelry were all taken by the Santa Barbara County Sheriff to repay creditors. There was no more wealth, no status, no friends left. He would die a broken man.

But I no longer needed a mentor.

Trudi and I worked well together, and we worked hard. Because we could generate fees for our range of services, and because we had shown the banks that The Carey Group was debt-free and generating new deals, we thrived.

When we got married, Trudi made it clear that she wanted to have children. I was older now, more mature, and all my "work-arounds" were working beautifully. I was ready to be the father I had once, secretly, failed to be.

As I held my first son in my arms, I could not share the memories of once holding Tanya the same way. And when our second son was born, I managed to convince myself that this new life—focused upon our financial success, parenting, and an active Santa Barbara social life—was all that mattered.

By the time our net worth passed the million-dollar mark, the lonely, lost, frightened boy from Hoboken finally had the financial security of his dreams. I was wealthy. I coached my boys' youth sports teams. I had friends among the social elite.

I had painted over the past with the colors of financial success and community respectability. I had won the race.

But for reasons I didn't understand, I needed to hear "What's your name?" again.

I had learned nothing.

The Demon wasn't satisfied.

Tom G. Carey & Tanya Laeger

Tanya: Bumpkins

By the time I was nine, we had moved several times, from one house to another, always to smaller and smaller towns. As if Centralia hadn't been small enough, we eventually landed in a rural area a half hour's drive to the nearest traffic light.

A single-wide mobile home on ten acres. We were on our way to becoming bona fide country bumpkins. My stepfather Dennis, with his charm and undeniable insistence, had convinced my mother that this was "the good life" where they could raise a family far from the materialistic influences of city folk. He spent his days working with logging crews while Mom kept the home fires burning and made sure she had a hot meal waiting for him each night.

My mother committed herself to making it all work, and work she did. She planted an acre of vegetable gardens, became expert at canning fruit and vegetables for the winters, and shared the work of tending to a handful of livestock. The effort apparently agreed with her, because she delivered two babies in a span of just 11 months.

I now had a brother and a sister to play with, my very own living baby dolls, and I enjoyed it immensely. They were now the apple of my stepfather's eye, his pride and joy. I knew my mother loved me, but now she had two children who depended on her for everything, as babies and toddlers do, and she had a husband who commanded the respect of all within his purview. It was obvious to everyone who knew Dennis Winters that you can take the man out of the SEALs, but you can't take the SEALs out of the man.

With a growing family to support, Dennis turned in his chainsaw and logging boots to become a deputy sheriff. It was a seamless transition for him, going from the military to logging to law enforcement. Now he could wear his sheriff's uniform with the same pride and bearing he had as a SEAL. Extraordinarily fit and confident, no one ever looked better behind that badge.

As he had in the military, my new dad now carried a gun. Everywhere he went, he was in authority, in charge. It was obvious he loved the concept of protecting the innocent and putting the bad guys behind bars. But the daily life of a cop isn't the sort of work one leaves at the office; it follows you home and goes with you wherever you may be.

As a ten year-old, dinner table stories of drugs, prostitution, and domestic violence only served to make me more anxious than ever. Because Dennis was often gone from home for extended days and nights with no indication of where he was, he bought my mother a police scanner so she could hear the minute-by-minute play-by-play of police work in real time. Our lives became centered around my stepfather's crime-busting adventures, and I became even more fearful about the world and my place in it.

Having been raised as he was, my stepfather's interest in traditional family values was diametrically opposed to my mother's. Thanksgiving and Christmas had always meant a great deal to her. That meant decorations, wonderful home cooking, and having the family gathered together. To Dennis, the Holidays only meant an opportunity to work a lucrative double-time shift. He always tried to make extra income whenever he could, because it was a long time between monthly paychecks and money was at the root of many marital conflicts.

Mom and Dennis had come from wildly different backgrounds, and those disparities were never more apparent than at Christmas. My mother would go all out preparing lavish gifts and home-baked goodies for all our relatives, friends, and neighbors while my stepfather would slam the door in the face of any carolers foolish enough to show up spreading holiday cheer. This isn't to say he never tried. One Christmas he actually gave my mother a present: a gun that he wanted for himself. My dad thought it was hilarious; my mother was not amused.

All the country living came to an end when I was 11 years old. My stepfather—on patrol in the town a half hour away—called to inform us that a prison escapee was headed to our house to kill the family of the man who had arrested him. That man had been Dennis. My mother and I grabbed my baby brother and sister and we locked ourselves in the back bedroom of the single-wide. With my mother sitting on the bed holding a shotgun, we waited for a violent prison escapee to knock

70

down the door, my anxiety was palpable. No one ever came, but between that threat and a roaming cougar eating our newborn piglets, my mother demanded we move back into town. The matter was closed if they were going to stay married.

I would soon learn that it didn't matter where we lived. I would not be safer in the same house with him.

Not safer at all.

Tom G. Carey & Tanya Laeger

Tom: **Patterns**

We lived in a spectacular custom-built home we had designed, located in Hope Ranch, one of Santa Barbara's most exclusive enclaves. Our neighbors included billionaires and celebrities. The country club was within walking distance. Our young sons both attended the area's most exclusive private school. We were involved in the city's active arts and charitable organizations. Our business was profitable and growing.

The future could not have been brighter for the Carey family.

And every day had become a living lie.

Our twelve years working together to build The Carey Group often put Trudi and me in competitive positions, as her need to control every aspect of our business—motivated, no doubt by witnessing her father's downward spiral into bankruptcy—began to bleed over into our family life. Having a disagreement over a project's loan rates at the office was one thing; bringing that conversation home to the dinner table and extending it into truly domestic matters created tensions that eventually made their way to the bedroom.

We weren't in love any more. We were in an endless negotiation. My lifelong issues with dyslexia put me at a disadvantage when faced with Trudi's hyper-verbal style and rapid-fire analytical skills. The girl I loved, the woman I married, the mother of my treasured sons had, in many ways, become an adversary.

I was sinking into an emotional pit with no bottom. My insecurities were surfacing, and my need for love wherever and however I could find it clouded my days. The paint on the canvas of my life was fading, and I needed to find some passion to bring it back to life.

"What's your name?" made my needy, narcissistic heart jump once again.

Her name was Catherine. A tall, willowy blonde, active in real estate sales, with her license hanging in a prominent local brokerage. Innuendo crept into our business conversations. Lingering gazes across conference tables surrounded by professional associates became a game. Inappropriate touches were not declined. It was an entertaining, ego-stroking challenge and infidelity was the prize.

Catherine filled the needs of the little boy from Hoboken, flattering me when I needed praise, loving me when I needed affection.

An illicit relationship serves many purposes. Aside from the obvious satisfactions of lust and the heart-pounding excitement of clandestine sexual encounters, it was a true test of my lifelong "work around" skills. As much as the sheer thrill of it all, there is great pride in being able to get away with it, to pull it off. To lie and not be found out.

The all-consuming energy of an affair either wanes or it becomes twisted into a perverted version of true romance borne of self-love. We kid ourselves into thinking that the passion is the truth, and nobody was able to kid himself more than the insecure boy from Hoboken.

Life with Trudi both at work and at home was a play, a performance. I was an expert at going through the motions, as I had been for more than a decade of marriage. Falsehoods and deception became my norm.

Behind the eyes of the man I saw each morning in the bathroom mirror, I was aware I had never been fully truthful with Trudi. She had zero knowledge of the daughter I had abandoned, who was now a teenager. Only a sociopath can escape the pangs of conscience, but I manipulated my conscience into believing that my affair with Catherine had a purpose; it fulfilled me at a time when Trudi could not. Therefore, the Demon reasoned, my behavior was helpful for all concerned, a necessary adjunct to our lives.

But even that rationalization and self-manipulation could not disguise the fact that I was obsessed with desire, with the forbidden. Catherine was playing her part, providing erotic distraction and passionate justification to assuage her own needs as well as mine. Our shared emotions were exciting and they were a hollow lie.

At night, I lay next to the mother of my children, waiting for her to fall asleep so that I could slip into the bathroom to call my lover. Catherine would say the words that would make me feel safe. She would tell me if she was being faithful to me, if she was with another lover, or if she was in bed with her husband.

She picked up on the first ring. "What's wrong?"

"Nothing. I just wanted to hear your voice," I said.

"When can I see you?" She was as reckless as I.

"I'll meet you at the apartment tomorrow at ten-thirty." Having vacant properties around town made getting together easy. "I'll dream of you tonight," I said. I silently returned the phone receiver to its cradle.

I slid quietly under the sheets, not daring to disturb my sleeping wife. Hugging my side of the bed, I convinced myself that I wasn't being unfaithful. I was just doing what I needed to do to fill a void, to feel some intimacy with someone, to know I was loved by *someone*.

Sleep was out of the question. I was too busy calculating the odds, imagining scenarios. I'd already been married and divorced twice before. Trudi and I had done the marriage counselor thing, and I'd artfully obfuscated and lied through every one of our pointless sessions with the nodding therapist.

It was a simple problem that, in my ego-maniacal state, I was confident I could solve. It was really just a matter of identifying the right pattern and then coming up with a nice little "work around" to put everything in the right place. The pieces of the pattern were clear: My two sons. Our gorgeous home. A successful business. Our community reputation. A tolerant wife. A lustful lover.

I just had to put all the pieces in the right place and hold them together with my dishonesty.

But I would soon discover that time is the enemy of lies.

The Demon would be exposed.

Tom G. Carey & Tanya Laeger

Tanya: PG-13

I was 47 years old when my husband Ron suggested that I share the details of the many challenges I had faced up to that point in my life. In Ron's ministry, we had seen many people struggle with forgiveness and the devastating effects its absence had on their lives. Ron was presenting a series of talks on forgiveness and thought it would be a stellar idea if I would be the last to speak about it. He thought it would be good for me to share my personal "journey to forgiveness." Then he asked me a difficult question: was I ready to forgive?

I was. Ron asked if I would be willing to share my story the following week, on a Thursday. Friday and Saturday I wrote out all the details I could recall in an effort to gain closure and forever draw the curtain on that chapter of my life.

In order to give myself some objective distance from the painful truth of my story, I wrote it in story form, complete with props; a suitcase, clothes, and shoes would represent the difficult emotions I had always felt but had never had the words to describe. Once the words were down on paper, I was ready to stand as a woman of faith to tell my story and to offer forgiveness to a father I didn't know.

Part of that story involves my childhood living with my mother and stepfather. In preparing to tell my story, I trembled with the same fear I felt when I was a child living with my mother and stepfather. I knew that the periodic bouts of anxiety I continued to suffer as an adult had a source, that I had unpacked baggage—my emotional suitcase filled with fear, insecurity, and rejection—still tucked away in the darkness and dust of the attic in my heart.

My knees literally began to shake and the butterflies in my stomach felt more like caged canaries trying to escape as I stood in front of the congregation that day. These were people I knew, and who knew me and my beloved husband. I nervously began telling my story with a disclaimer: *"This is going to be a PG-13 testimony with some adult themes."* Those hesitant words did little to calm my fluttering heart as I stood there in front the silent crowd. But I had prayed and knew the Lord would strengthen me for this very moment. My goal was to give encouragement to others who had struggled with unforgiveness and to show how God can redeem even the darkest moments. Together, He and I would turn on the attic light. He would help me say the words I had not dared to speak for nearly four decades.

"I never really felt a part of my stepfather's home. I constantly fought the distinct feeling that I was the old, ugly discarded wrapping paper that came along with the package in which my mom was the prize. I always felt on edge and on alert when I was in that home.

"We lived in a sexually charged house. Porn magazines came every month in a brown paper cover. We lived in an average house for the time, five people, one bathroom. The bathroom didn't have a lock on it. But right inside, there was a drawer you could pull out and it would block the door from opening all the way. My dad would always throw a fit, along with a slew of colorful language about my blocking the door in the bathroom. He never shut the door. For some reason, even though I was a super compliant kid, I continued to block the door even though it made him angry.

"I was in the bathroom one day taking a bath. No one else was in the house when he came home. Dad tried to get into the bathroom, but I had the door blocked with the open cabinet drawer. A few choice words, and he left. I was relieved.

"Then he came back with a kitchen knife. He started to jimmy the drawer through the open door slot and finally slid the drawer closed. I was paralyzed with fear. Screaming on the inside, but no sound came out. I knew this was not going to end well. I was right.

"That day, I learned the world is indeed unsafe. The people who are supposed to protect you don't. I felt powerless, ashamed, embarrassed, guilty. Those were just some of the conflicting feelings I packed into my suitcase. The man I thought was supposed to be a protector had left a young, vulnerable, scared little girl even more so. In looking back, I know it could have been worse, and I'm forever grateful that was the only time that happened, although it didn't relieve the constant fear of something happening again. Living in fear is wearying to a 13-year-old soul. I tightly shut that suitcase and packed it away, back up in that dusty attic where nobody could ever find it."

The people who heard me speak those words in Ron's church sat silently listening, for I had much more to tell them that day. I was thankful I couldn't see into the eyes of those gathered due to the bright stage lights; otherwise I might not have had the courage to continue.

I was sixteen when my mother gave me what I thought was a perplexing and unusual gift. I had not been someone who read much for the sheer joy of reading, although I earned good grades throughout school because I loved learning, just not having to do it in a room full of other kids.

So when Mom gave me a copy of "The Living Bible," I was somewhat perplexed. Our family had not attended church or observed any religious holidays other than Christmas, so getting a Bible for my sixteenth birthday—usually a milestone birthday for girls approaching adulthood—was completely unexpected.

That night, after enjoying a chocolate-on-chocolate birthday cake baked by my mother, I retreated to my room and opened the enormous book. Page one: The Book of Genesis. I was immediately drawn to the words on the page, impressed by how beautifully written it was, how the language seemed to flow so effortlessly off the page.

I knew absolutely nothing about the Bible, Christianity, or any other religious belief when I opened that book. It was filled with fascinating stories, intriguing plots, and compelling characters traveling among exotic places I had never even heard about. I had always approached my schoolwork in an orderly, structured way, and here were carefully organized accounts detailing the creation of the universe with a logic that made much more sense to me than the speculative "big bang" scientific theories with which I was being taught in science class.

By the time I was halfway through reading Genesis, something inside me stirred. I wondered "If there really is a God out there, somewhere, please love me."

It was a plea for a connection, for at bedtime I had eventually stopped whispering "Good night, Daddy. Please don't forget me," in the hope that somehow my whispers would reach the ears of the father who had left me behind a decade earlier. But Tom never heard my words, knew nothing of my need for his love or for the security of his protective arms around me, arms that I imagined would have shielded me from this unpredictable world I was in.

Memories of my father were fading, retreating into the mist of passing years. I had no photographs, no mementos of any kind. There was no memento to reassure me that at one time in my life, my father had truly loved me. Instead, the recesses of my mind slowly closed over my childhood memories, and I stopped wondering where he was, what he was doing, or if he even remembered he had a little girl who thought he was the moon and the stars. Even with an occasional thunderstorm of anger, the longing to be loved by him would stay hidden in the deep recesses of my heart.

I've heard it said that time heals all wounds. Sometimes it just makes us stop feeling the sting of their pain. Eventually we forget we have old wounds and we bury the memory of them, often because we have fresh ones to deal with. My memories of my father were buried in those old wounds now. Buried, forgotten, but always there.

My thoughts turned to the possibility that someone could love me, and that love was mine without limits, without recrimination, without judgment. I only had to be open to this love, to accept it as it was offered to me, fully, completely, unconditionally. If there was indeed a Heavenly Father and He loved me, then I would know my life would have meaning.

I needed someone to trust, someone to love.

Would that someone be God the Father?

Or would that someone be the father I no longer remembered?

Tom: Pretender

I ignored the irony of it all.

The offices of The Carey Group were something of a "family affair," with Trudi a controlling force behind her desk, a small but loyal staff headed by our long-time office manager Sylvia, and myself out in the field, closing deals and supervising ongoing projects.

I frequently had good reason to be out of the office, and those reasons were often vaguely communicated to Sylvia. The less Sylvia knew about my actual whereabouts, the less Trudi would know. Communication between my wife and our office manager was constant and instantaneous.

I had to be careful what I told Sylvia if my trysts with Catherine were to continue undetected.

But men and women are, as they say, quite different. Where a man is confident he has covered his tracks and left no evidence behind, a woman only needs to walk into a room to know something is amiss. In my mind, there was no reason for Trudi to suspect anything was going on. By then, however, my mind was hardly a dependable gauge of reality.

Trudi confronted me with her suspicions that I was hiding something, that I was acting oddly, suspiciously.

We made arrangements to attend marriage counseling, both as a couple, and individually. We had too much at stake to simply let our marriage fall apart.

Initially, issues of control were the focus of our therapy sessions. Our therapist soon had a handle on the fact that Trudi and I had come from wildly disparate backgrounds. The therapist was encouraging me to accept the concept of my "inner child," a boy seeking his father's approval and hurting others in my life as I walked that steep uphill path. Of course, making any progress toward understanding required a level of honesty that I wasn't prepared to approach.

Honesty was simply of no value to me. The truth was not an option.

I fully understood what points the therapist was making; I simply didn't care to embrace them. To do so would mean unveiling my shell-hard narcissism and selfishness.

For months, I pretended to participate in these therapy sessions. 45 minutes of listening and then responding in the most inconsequential ways I could. My mind was rarely in the room with Trudi and the doctor. I was counting the minutes until I would be in my car, driving to a secret destination to be with the woman who would hold me in a passionate embrace and who would not ask questions.

I was simply getting my bottomless need for love and acceptance from somewhere else. I was addicted to the thrill of the lies and the insidious excitement of the illicit passion that was mine whenever I picked up the phone to call my lover.

As we attended multiple counseling sessions each week, I continued seeing Catherine when the office staff was told I was "out on appointments." All I had to do to maintain the status quo of my deceitful relationship, apparently, was to continue painting over the canvas of my marriage with another layer of lies.

This is not to say I was ignorant of the truth. I just wasn't going to admit to the pain I had caused others, to confess to the truth of my ruthless ambition, to my impenetrable insecurities, to my obvious talent for manipulation. I wasn't forced to face those ugly facts, so I didn't.

But when the underlying colors on a canvas haven't yet had the time to dry before more layers are urgently brushed over them, pigments run together and the picture distorts. If the canvas does dry, it is riddled with cracks.

Truth, I would soon come to realize, flows in an unpredictable course as it seeps through those cracks.

But my truth would not come seeping. It would hit me like a tsunami.

Tanya: Crockpot

A s memories of early childhood fade, they're replaced by the more indelible impressions of adolescence.

The past becomes more present. Memories feel more immediate. Some, unfortunately, are never forgotten, never diluted by the passage of years.

"Along with the abuse came its twin, 'the threat.' Mine was specific: if you tell anyone, you will destroy our family.

"Well, I loved my Mom and my brother and sister and I certainly didn't want to be the one to destroy my family. So into the suitcase went the weight of responsibility for keeping the dark family secret. We were 'the house next door,' the average American family, except that we had a family secret, one that I didn't dare share with anybody because I didn't want to be the one who destroyed our family."

By now, my quivering voice had become more confident. There was something liberating about sharing our family secrets with these people we'd known and who had been such a source of love and encouragement Over the previous weeks, my husband had asked other people to share their personal stories of forgiveness as well. Each had a compelling life story that riveted our attention and allowed us the privilege to peek inside the complexity of the human soul.

My husband was aware that I'm not a particularly trusting person, that I don't trust anyone until they somehow prove themselves as trustworthy. Ron knew I had that suitcase in my attic, that I had issues of unresolved conflict and insecurities, and was not particularly inclined to forgive the two men in my life who had rejected me and from whom I was emotionally estranged. Now Ron was asking me to share how I had worked through my younger years of estrangement and rejection, how I had processed my pain and finally granted my father and stepfather forgiveness. It was at this point that I discovered forgiveness and trust are two different things. I could truly forgive and acknowledge what I was forgiving, but trust is something that can only be restored over time.

Ron stood before our church to explain that some people are "microwave forgivers" and others are "crockpot forgivers," and that I was the latter. And so, in preparing for this day before those seated in the church, I had journaled my deepest pain, writing down who I was forgiving, what I was forgiving them for, and how I had processed my pain with considerable specificity.

Simply writing it all down became cathartic. I identified the painful episodes, one by one, and in so doing I felt the pain again and was able to release it. It was a moment of taking responsibility not for the events, but for the emotional reactions I attached to them. I would no longer be the helpless victim forever in search of others to love me or to fulfill me.

I bared my soul that day to our beloved church. Looking back now, I realize it brought a deeper understanding to my reserved, quiet nature. Those who heard me that day learned that even a pastor's wife can have a tumultuous past, struggle with life's circumstances, and yet strive to live a life worthy of God's redeeming grace.

"My Mom was always trying to get me to have a better relationship with my dad, to spend more time with him. One day he took me and his best friend's daughter out for 'bonding time.' He drove us out into the woods, told me to stay in the truck, and he took my friend for a walk through the trees.

"I learned that day that I was helpless to protect others. Into the suitcase went the hoodie of powerlessness and shame. I knew she was being violated and there was nothing I could do but wait until it was all over.

"They both came out of the woods. Dad climbed in behind the wheel. I was in the middle. My friend sat beside me. Everyone looked forward, staring through the windshield, with not a single word spoken on the ride back home. My life as the keeper of dark secrets continued.

"The next year, after seeing a film in PE class that talked about abuse and the need for victims to tell someone, I churned inside for days. I finally summoned the courage to tell my Mom. I was relieved to have finally shared the dark secret. Her reaction was disbelief, but when she confronted him, he confessed. It was the first and only time I

ever saw this former SEAL cry. He swore he would never do such a thing again. My sense of relief was complete.

"But a half hour later, out in the driveway, he looked me in the eye and said 'If you ever need 20 bucks, you know where to come and what to do to get it.' My fleeting moment of relief was gone. Now I packed a garment of pure distrust into my attic suitcase. I realized that emotional apologies weren't to be trusted, and neither were the people who made them. Fear and trepidation would now be my constant companions."

Until I spoke to our church that day, I had been a caterpillar tightly wrapped in a cocoon of unrecognized thoughts, feelings, and emotions. Once acknowledged, I was able to unravel the cocoon and be transformed. I could fly into the future unhindered by the fears and insecurities of the past. I discovered that true forgiveness gives flight to freedom and the ability to truly have empathy for others who have gone through distressing things in their lives as well.

My step-father had passed away by the time I spoke in church that day, and I was approaching a place of true forgiveness for the father who had abandoned me as a three year-old. It had come over a span of many years, and I never thought I would see my father again. I was good with that. It has been said that "forgiveness is a solo; reconciliation, a duet."

I would be playing a solo, and I was satisfied to let things go at that. I would let the past go.

But the past was not ready to let me go.

• • • •

Every couple of years or so, my mother Marilyn would plan a family vacation. We would visit her parents in Oxnard either during summer vacation or during the Christmas holiday school break.

It was 1980, and I was sixteen and looking forward to seeing my grandparents. We only saw them once every year or two, so with each visit I learned more about these virtual strangers who were my grandparents. I had always fostered fond childhood memories of the warm sand of California's beaches, so the non-stop drive with my stepfather behind the wheel driving with the end goal in mind, with the absolute minimum number of stops for gas and hasty bathroom breaks was well worth it.

Arriving at my grandparents' house—standing squarely in the middle of a "Brady Bunch" neighborhood—felt like we were pulling into a scene reminiscent of a Hallmark greeting card. Clean architecture of the mid-1970s, manicured lawns and sun that greeted us every morning upon rising. So different from the grey skies of the Northwest.

Most of the time, I walked around in a fog, going through the motions wherever I was without really being "present," because I wasn't. I suppose my distracted, disconnected persona earned the nickname my stepdad gave me: Doodle-O. I hated that name; I would have preferred a name like "Princess" or some other endearing label. But Doodle-O? There was nothing endearing about that, just a reminder that I moved at molasses speed.

In reality, however, I was a pondering dreamer, always imagining I was somewhere else, and so I navigated my life shrouded in fear and insecurity, avoiding the genuine dangers of the outside world, living my private interior life.

At my grandparents', we were always welcomed warmly. I was repeatedly hugged with the usual "My, haven't you grown?" to which I would respond by blushing with an innocent shrug. My grandmother and mother did their best to maintain an affectionate façade, but even at sixteen I could feel the tension between them. Their pretense of sincerity did a poor job of casting a veil over mutual resentments, a relationship dynamic with which I was all too familiar. But at least I was in the company of others, which forced Mom and Dennis into more relaxed postures of tolerant civility with one another.

My grandfather worked at the nearby Point Magu Naval Air Station, just south of Oxnard. I never understood what he actually did here, but he always seemed to have his hands on the latest technology of the day. With all the relatives gathered in his living room, he proudly fired up the newest home movie projection equipment, and as we settled in to watch scenes from our family's past. I watched with intrigue the faces of aunts, uncles, and cousins with whom I wasn't familiar, but who were called "family."

For me, it was curious to hear the recollections of those around me as they talked about the people in these flickering black-and-white images who had a connection to me. I was fascinated by the faces of young and old members of past generations up on the screen.

And then I saw the image of my mother. She was sitting on the lap of a stranger wearing blue jeans, brown loafers, and a white t-shirt with a pack of cigarettes rolled up in the sleeve. He was smoking a cigarette. The two of them smiled, beaming.

Suddenly, the room became silent.

"Wow, Mom. Who's that man?" I asked, a question borne of mere curiosity. It was obviously a relationship from her younger years.

My grandmother reacted first, tossing a slew of profanities as she left the room, indicating she was done with family movie night. Her reaction was curious and bewildered me. I looked to my mother, waiting for an answer.

"Tanya, that is your father."

To say I could have been knocked over with a feather would be inaccurate. I could have been knocked over by the breeze made by a passing feather. I hadn't seen my father or any photos of him for 13 years, since the day he left me standing there in the yard of our Oxnard apartment, with me dressed in my white patent-leather Mary Janes.

The home movies continued flickering, but I saw nothing. I heard nothing. The awkward silence that filled the room felt like a deafening roar.

"Would you like to meet him?" Mom asked.

My face went hot. I didn't know what to say. Everyone in the room was looking at me, waiting for a response, an answer.

"Sure," I said. I just wanted to see his face, unable to imagine the pain that would follow.

Tom G. Carey & Tanya Laeger

Tom: Addicted

I thought I was actually pretty convincing in our marriage counseling sessions, artfully pretending early on that I was revealing everything to my wife and to our therapist. At times, I thought I may have missed my calling. I could have been quite the actor with my ability to convincingly portray a character I was not. I told myself I was doing a great job in our sessions, always ready to compromise. I appeared to be a real giver, and I was proud of the appearance.

As months of sessions wore on, I began to understand just how many layers of dark colors I had brushed onto the canvas of my life and how I had always lived a lie. It was becoming apparent to my inner child that I was far from a giver or a compromiser. I was actually a skilled manipulator with the ability to justify almost anything others might perceive as a selfish shortcoming.

The question I began to ask myself was "why am I going to all this trouble to hide the truth?" Many of our sessions devolved into accusations, explanations, excuses, justifications, which often generated real anger on my part and tears on Trudi's part.

The therapist, while not seeing through all of the layers of paint beneath which my true self was hiding, eventually forced me to understand the genuine nature of my narcissism. I began to admit my feelings of anger and fear, and the resentments I held for my father. Sexual and intellectual insecurities became a focus of inquiry. I listened carefully to each question in order to fashion acceptable answers that wouldn't expose the real truth behind my lies.

I began to wonder just how much our therapist was seeing, whether he could tell when I was lying or when I was telling the truth. With each question, I heard the voice of the boy from Hoboken whispering "don't expose yourself."

I heard the word narcissist, but I couldn't allow that label to be applied to me. That would have required an honesty that I wouldn't have use for anytime during this marriage.

The subterfuge would be maintained, so I went through the motions of the dutiful husband fighting to preserve his marriage and his relationship with his two sons. My ability to love truly and openly was firmly anchored to "What's your name?" and I wasn't hearing it within this marriage.

Lies of omission persisted. I made no mention of my first marriage to Marilyn or of Tanya, the girl we had together. In my mind, of course, after more than a decade of marriage to Trudi during which she had no knowledge of my first child, there was no point in telling her now.

Unless the point was truth itself.

I threw Trudi and the therapist a bone. I confessed to my ongoing affair with Catherine. I expected Trudi would be hurt, but because we had two sons, a business, and lifestyle, I thought she just might swallow her pride and suck it up. My marital transgression was, after all, fairly typical for the times, and I thought "the times" might be a fairly slick justification. With an entire session devoted to my admission of guilt and a nice, thick layer of fairly credible apologies slathered over the whole thing like so much greasy paint on the canvas of my life, I thought things might just settle down.

· · · ·

When you have your own business and significant financial resources, finding the time for extra-marital activities isn't difficult. There's always a meeting at the city planning office, the building department, a visit to a job site, or an out-of-town client to wine and dine. Mobile phones were at their infancy, so communication with an illicit lover was only a pay phone away.

I left for the office early. I was hoping to get some work done before noon so that I could leave the office early and rendez-vous with Catherine, the woman who makes me feel safe, loved.

Getting out of the office before Trudi came in was essential if I was going to avoid her questions about my schedule. Our counseling sessions—pointless with my constant deception—had alerted Trudi to my "former" affair, and her newfound vigilance was now nearly manic.

When I pulled into the office parking lot, I saw Sylvia sitting at her desk by the window. I needed to call Catherine to set our meeting time, so I walked across the street to use the coffee shop's pay phone. Our conversation was brief, but breathless. We arranged to meet that afternoon. I wanted her. I wanted it all: my business, my family, my reputation.

Commitment, integrity, and honesty just weren't part of my equation. They certainly had nothing to do with what I wanted, because the Demon wants it all.

I walked back to the office, secure in the knowledge that within hours I would be in the arms of the woman who truly loved me, who made me feel safe.

It was early. Sylvia and I were the only ones in the office. Trudi wouldn't be in for another two hours.

The phone rang. The business day was starting early. My intercom buzzed and I heard Sylvia's voice. "There is someone named Marilyn on line one. She won't tell me what she wants. Do you want to take it?"

I had not heard that name in more than a decade. "Yes, I'll take it." My fingers went suddenly cold as the blood drained out of them.

I kept my voice low. This would undoubtedly be a very private conversation, but I didn't want Sylvia to suspect anything secretive might be going on, and the last thing I wanted was for her to be caught in the middle of my lies. I knew that when she arrived, Trudi would immediately ask if there were any calls. If, somehow, I could make Marilyn's call appear to be from a vendor or a client's secretary, there would be no uncomfortable questions for Sylvia to deal with.

Marilyn didn't waste any time and came right to the point. "We're here in Oxnard visiting my parents. Your daughter would like to meet her biological father."

My heart stopped.

Did I want to see the daughter I had said goodbye to so long ago? Yes.

Could I hide this from Trudi? Sure. After all, I was hiding a hot and heavy affair right under her nose.

Could I continue lying about all of it? No doubt.

"I'll meet you for lunch at the Port Royal Restaurant in the Oxnard marina. Does that work for you?" I knew the area well. It was the perfect spot for a very private meeting.

Marilyn said she and Tanya would be there to meet me at noon.

"One thing, Marilyn. I need to talk to you before I see Tanya."

One of my clients was a developer in the Oxnard area, and he owned the Port Royal. It was the perfect cover if anyone in the office learned where I was going for lunch that day. With just a little bit of luck, no one will ever know I'm meeting my daughter for lunch, and no one will ever know I even have a daughter at all.

I hung up the phone hoping the bald-faced lie I was about to tell Sylvia would not be apparent. I averted my eyes, appearing to busy myself with paperwork as I off-handedly remarked "I have a meeting in Oxnard. I'll be gone most of the day."

It would truly be a full day indeed. First a brief reunion with Marilyn and the daughter I hadn't seen since she was a toddler. Then my get-together with Catherine. I had already done all the work I would do that day. "Tell Trudi I have to meet someone in the Oxnard Planning Department for lunch."

I was so good at lying that this all seemed to flow from my lips casually, with natural insouciance. I felt a moment's guilt over lying so boldly to Sylvia, using her as my cover with Trudi. My twisted logic told me that my meeting with Marilyn and Tanya was part of a family secret that had nothing to do with Trudi, my two sons, my business, or my friends and associates. So this was a lie that was only supporting a secret that was in the best interests of everyone. I was protecting my family. What better reason for a lie could there be?

Sylvia, however, held a special place in my life. She was a hard-working young woman whom I had met while working for Santa Barbara's leading real estate development company, where I had learned so much. It was there, while finalizing a cost analysis report I had drafted, that she came into my office, saw my work in progress, and looked me right in the eye with "Do you know you're dyslexic?"

I had heard the term, but I never understood its implications or how it could possibly apply to me. Because Sylvia had worked for the local dyslexia institute as a volunteer, she recognized my pronounced use of homophones and phonetics as a key indicator of the affliction. She handed me a pamphlet with "Read this. You're dyslexic, Tom."

Learning from Sylvia that what I endured every day was an inherited trait experienced by millions of others was liberating. The boy from Hoboken wasn't stupid or slow or lazy like all those teachers had repeatedly told his parents.

I soon learned there were reasons for some of the decisions I had made throughout my life, for my constant need for "work arounds." There was now an explanation for myself. A large right brain hemisphere had gifted me with artistic, athletic, and mechanical skills that made me a creative problem solver with 3-D visualization and intuitive people skills. It was a serious reading disability on the one hand, but on the other it allowed me to achieve unusual success in my field.

I had inherited an anomalous chromosome #6 from a father who had released his own frustrations through the same anger, defensiveness, and insecurities which became the foundation of my ability to manipulate the truth and everyone around me. Sylvia had taught me much about my disability, and I owed her the truth.

But lying and getting away with lies is addictive, a drug as strong as any other.

So that morning, I lied to Sylvia as I lied to myself.

• • • •

I drove down U.S. 101, heading south from Santa Barbara toward Oxnard. It's a uniquely beautiful drive, with the vast Pacific stretching out toward the horizon. The Channel Islands appear close enough to reach out and touch. Surfers perform their aquatic gymnastics just off the shoulder of the highway, pelicans skimming the tops of waves behind them. It's a thirty mile drive like few others on the continent.

I saw none of it.

I drove in silence, staring straight ahead at the four-lane road. I didn't listen to the radio. My mind was racing, then stumbling, then stalling, then accelerating as I tried to form some idea of what I could possibly say to a teenage girl in search of her father, in search of *me*.

From the 101, I took the Highway 1 exit onto Pacific Coast Highway, a shortcut through Oxnard toward the harbor and the Port Royal restaurant. The weather was straight out of a Chamber of Commerce playbook, a warm clear day. My car had excellent air conditioning, yet my palms had gone clammy, my mind unable to focus on anything but the obvious question: *Why does she want to see me now?*

There were other questions I heard in the recesses of my mind that I couldn't answer : *Why am I making this trip? Why is it so important for me to see the little girl I've kept hidden for so long? What will I say? What can I possibly say that will explain anything?*

More questions than answers.

I pulled into the restaurant parking lot early, at 11:30. I had thirty minutes before I would see the little girl I had left standing in front of our apartment, dressed in her blue coat, waving me goodbye. I walked to the dock in front of the restaurant to watch boats sailing past. The water was calm with a freshening breeze, perfect conditions for good sailors to maintain a steady course.

I had never stayed the course, sailing through my life erratically, abandoning a child to swim uncharted waters on her own.

Now I was about to be tossed into those waters myself.

Tanya: Trembling

A n unsettled brew of anxiety and anticipation percolated inside as I awakened knowing I was about to see my real father for the first time in 13 years. Before my head was even off the pillow that morning, I trembled with questions that couldn't be answered by this sixteen year-old.

Where has he been all this time? What if he doesn't like me? What if I don't measure up? What if he thinks I'm ugly and never wants to see me again? What if I say or do something wrong and make him leave all over again?

We pulled into the parking lot, in front of a large, elegant restaurant festooned with nautical regalia. My mother parked the car, spotted someone approaching in her rear view mirror. "Just wait here," she said as she opened her door and slid out from behind the wheel.

I did. I waited right there, staring straight ahead through the windshield. I shook with tense anticipation. I was so anxious to see what he looked like, but I was too scared to turn around and see for myself.

Behind me, Mom and Tom stood by the rear bumper. They had not laid eyes on each other since the turbulent and nasty divorce. Tension in their muffled voices failed to cut through the distancing years.

He wanted to know if I had been legally adopted by Dennis Winters, my stepfather. I knew the answer to that because I had once asked my stepfather if he had adopted me since I was using his last name. His response was that he had not adopted me, reasoning that if anything ever happened between my mom and him, he would not question that I would go with my mother. I interpreted that, again, as the fact that I was just not worth fighting for.

Mom bristled at Tom's question. "What's the difference?"

Tom explained that if I had been adopted, he would not want to see me, for fear it would only complicate things further. My mother raised her voice. An edge of anger. She didn't bring me here for this. He had agreed to see me, and she was not going to let him get out of it, not this time.

Mom and I walked into the ornately-decorated restaurant. I'm sure my eyes widened at the sight of elegant sailboats gliding down the channel, just outside the oversized dining room picture windows.

And then I saw him sitting in a booth against the windows. He stood when he saw us, and my knees trembled as we walked toward him.

An awkward smile, an outstretched hand. It was cold. He was as nervous as I was, very tall, blondish hair, blue eyes, fair skinned.

Imposing. A smile, but a serious smile.

As my mother and I sat in the plush leather booth, I was relieved to take the weight off my vibrating knees.

He sat across the table from me, and I immediately recognized my features in his face. I suddenly realized comments throughout my childhood about my resemblance to my mother were merely a kind distraction from the truth: I carried this man's DNA.

I was my father's daughter.

The conversation had a difficult, hesitant start.

We were both looking at each other, curious to see what depths were revealed in familiar-looking eyes.

I glanced away as the waitress came and brought us water with a slice of lemon stuck on the rim of the glass. Compared to what I was accustomed to, not having money to eat at anyplace other than fast food restaurants, and then only on rare occasion. I was frozen, looking at that lemon slice perched there.

My mother, her lips impatiently pursed from their brief parking lot exchange, tersely got the ball rolling. "Tom, this is your daughter, Tanya."

My chest was so tight I couldn't summon enough air to speak. I felt warm, wet droplets rolling down my sunburned cheeks. I was so ugly, so frightened, so out of place.

The waitress rescued me as she returned to take our lunch order. I wanted to be sure to order something that wouldn't be messy or too expensive. For some reason, I was always embarrassed to eat in front of other people. I would skip lunch at school and go home famished. When Ron and I started dating in high school, he thought I was to poor to afford the school lunches, and would offer to buy mine. "I'll have the fruit salad" is all I could get past the catch in my throat. I never noticed what he or my mother ordered.

It didn't matter.

We weren't going to do much eating.

Tom G. Carey & Tanya Laeger

Tom: Deaf

E veryone looks at the world through their own eyes. We see things differently, from our own point of view, carried down the river of our lives by our own perspectives and feelings.

I sat at that table facing Marilyn and Tanya, burdened by a lifetime of lies as recent as those I had told Sylvia that same morning. It was noon. I had plans to connect with Catherine later, after this lunch.

I looked at Marilyn, the woman I had once loved deeply yet betrayed with such cavalier abandon and who now clearly had no affection for me. Her words were pointed. "This is your daughter."

I looked at Tanya, the girl I had left behind but never forgotten. My guilt is no match for my self-absorption, for my own needs, yet I could not suppress the shame I felt looking into this beautiful girl's eyes. *What does she want?*

Perhaps it was the Demon playing tricks on me, dangling my ego in front of me as I was being swept into an emotional vortex that suddenly had me obsessed with wanting this girl to like me, to accept me as her loving father. I was wanting, but not giving anything.

Words came out of Tanya's mouth and I heard them. But the meaning behind them, their implication and the significance of our meeting was completely lost on me. My emotional IQ was at ground zero, such was my level of narcissism.

"I wanted to meet my biological father," are the words I heard. I didn't hear her need for understanding, for acceptance, for connection. I didn't hear the pain behind her every word because I was too concerned with my own.

I would eventually understand Tanya's unspoken cry for help. But on that day, the father whose DNA she carried was incurably deaf.

The waitress returned and lunch was served.

No one touched their food.

Sitting there across from Marilyn and Tanya, I struggled for words to express the shame and remorse I felt. I simply didn't have the ability to reveal the guilt I had always carried for walking out of the life of this lovely teenager whom I simply did not know.

Tanya was calm and reserved. She looked up from a ridiculously ornate salad and looked me straight in the eye. "I have a family. I don't want to cause any problems for you. I just wanted to meet you."

Ahh. An easy reprieve. I wasn't being held responsible for anything. I wasn't guilty at all. I had done the right thing and now all the justifications I had made for not being in my daughter's life were validated.

This confident, beautiful young lady is fine; she doesn't need me.

The waitress returned to clear our plates. We nodded and smiled at her in silence. The waitress presented Tanya's leftover salad packaged in a tin foil sculpture resembling a swan, a memento typical of a restaurant catering to vacationers and weekend visitors.

I sat patiently as I paid the check with a credit card. There was still plenty of time to make my appointment with Catherine.

"Thank you for lunch," Tanya said with unusual poise for a sixteen-year-old. Apparently, Marilyn had done a good job in the parenting department. She and Tanya pushed through the restaurant's glass doors and were gone.

My eyes welled up as I quietly wept.

"Are you okay?" the waitress asked.

"Sure. I'm fine," I said.

The lies would just not stop.

Tanya: Swans

The waitress brought our food, and my fruit salad was like nothing I had ever seen. Fast food restaurants never served anything in a pineapple bowl cut into the shape of a swan and packed with perfect triangles of fruit. There was not a seed or a piece of peel or rind to be seen. It was elegant and intimidating.

Eating any of it was out of the question. My stomach was churning as I tried hard to hold back uncontrollable tears. I discovered that it's hard to eat and cry at the same time. I looked at the fruit and touched none of it.

My father did almost all of the talking. His voice was deep, imposing. He seemed stern. He told me he was an architect, living in Santa Barbara. Although we had lived only 35 miles to the south when I was younger, I had never been to Santa Barbara. We knew its reputation as the privileged home of elites, but this was unfamiliar territory and would never be our playing field.

He talked about his work, telling us about several building projects he was working on. He told me he had paid for his college years by modeling and appearing in TV commercials. He was good-looking, and I melted into my seat, feeling awkward and ugly, knowing I was not exactly fashion model material.

At school, after early years of social awkwardness, crooked teeth, and an anorexic physique, I had become a cheerleader, but that didn't assuage my poor self image much. The eruption of Mount St. Helens had closed schools early that year, and without student body input, I was "elected" by the faculty which I suspected was reward for my angelic conduct and good grades.

Once my father had finished talking about his work projects, he asked me if I had any questions for him.

I did. "Do you have a family?" I asked.

He took in a short breath, then said he was married, and that she was an architect too. He deftly turned the conversation back to his work, but I had another question that simply fell out of my mouth with the inevitability of gravity.

"Do they know about me?" I was nothing if not terminally hopeful.

"No," he said. His tone closed the subject.

I felt the sting of rejection spiraling upward into my brain, words unnecessary as I computed the likelihood of him being ashamed of me, of regretting having fathered some random child who was not, nor ever would be, a part of his life. *Why wouldn't he tell his family about me?* If there was an answer to that question, I never heard it and would not have been able to process it if I had.

I wanted to tell him about our family, about living in Washington State, about my little brother and sister, about what had happened to me in the bathroom, about the frustration, shame, fear, and insecurities that were inside, that weren't the cheerleader, but were the components of the *real me*. My instinct was to let the welling up in my eyes have free rein, to let my tears speak to what my words could not, to let my emotions reveal themselves in deep sobs.

But I was in unfamiliar territory, sitting here in a fancy restaurant with salads shaped like exotic birds and white yachts drifting by on the other side of the window. I was a survivor of my own feelings because I had become an expert at keeping them in check, buried deep inside that suitcase that I had hidden away in the shadows of my emotional attic. As a child, I had been trained well by a former Navy SEAL who would sit on my chest, pin me down, and tickle me until my chest felt like it would explode. Pleading for release to no avail, I would be overpowered, gasping with claustrophobic panic and utter helplessness. Crying would only earn me more of the same, so I learned to create my reserved, always-in-control-and-perfectly-together persona. I developed a talent for disconnecting my emotions from words both heard and spoken.

And so I sat in front of my salad-swan in a comfy leather restaurant booth, never lifting the heavy curtain of my feelings or revealing the longing within my heart to connect in some sincere way with this stranger, my father.

As we left the restaurant and stepped into the bright light of the Southern California sun, my father asked me if I was planning to go to college. It felt like an odd question and a strange way, after having been apart for so many years, of wrapping up our father-daughter reunion.

I was stuck for an answer. Although I had excellent grades, there was no academic encouragement or interest in higher education to be found within the walls of our home. I had never even given a moment's thought as to what I might do with myself beyond high school graduation. My future had never been a topic of conversation, not even of my own.

Just before he turned to go, my father looked at me with eyes that mirrored my own and said "Please keep in touch."

Four words that changed my world, like a life ring thrown to my drowning heart. Those words ricocheted around the walls of my insecurities, spoken by my father in his deep voice with a sincerity that convinced me he wanted further contact with his little girl.

Climbing back into my mother's car, hope washed over me. I would soon be able to discover who my father really was, what he was like, if I was anything like him. I would find the path to a relationship with him. He would see who I was and what had become of that little blue-eyed pigtailed three-year-old girl, the one with the funny quirks and shy insecurities who had missed him every single day and night for the past thirteen years.

I would finally have an opportunity to learn about this father, this stranger, to see if I could re-enter his life and feel like his little girl.

· · · ·

I didn't want to appear too childish or over-anxious, so although I had started writing the letter to my father immediately, I worked on it for over a week before I sent it.

I've always been able to express myself better in writing than in person, taking great delight in finding just the right words and going over them repeatedly to make sure the cadence and rhythm flow perfectly and express the things I could never speak aloud.

I wrote and I rewrote.

I wanted every word of my letter to sound just right. I wrote about what my life and family were like. I wrote about myself—feeling strange doing so—describing who I was, the things I liked, and what I

felt inside. I wrote about everything a father should know...if he had not stayed away and been such a stranger.

Once the letter was finally done, I folded it perfectly and slid it into a clean, unwrinkled envelope. I was eager to show him he could be proud of me for something, and I enclosed a picture that had just been taken of me in my high school cheerleader's uniform.

Everything I hoped for and cared about was in that clean, smooth envelope. I thought a lot about where I should send it. Sending it to his house— where no one in his family even knew I existed—might be uncomfortable for him. I imagined the awkwardness a picture of a sixteen year-old girl in a cheerleading outfit tumbling out of my envelope onto the family dining room table.

I had a much better idea. Love wasn't part of the equation at this point, just curiosity and the desire to be loved.

I sent my letter to his office.

Tom: Exposed

The Santa Barbara office of The Carey Group was a cordial, friendly environment. Trudi and I were the heads of an active team of professionals who were, in many respects, a working family.

Trudi had been at the vanguard of interior business design, and created one of the earliest "open" office floor plans. No closed doors, no hush-hush meetings. The flow of information among team members and employees was the lifeblood of our daily operations.

The fact that Trudi and I had been seeing a marriage and family counselor since the early days of our marriage was no secret. Staffers were aware that I had had an affair, but since I had worked through all those issues in counseling, my unfaithful past was simply that: in the past, and not spoken of.

I had been taking great self-pride in my ability to navigate this transparent environment with the skill of a tightrope walker in a stiff wind. My affair with Catherine—which I had confessed to Trudi in our counseling sessions and was presumptively now filed away as my deeply regretted mid-life crisis for which I would be forever repentant—continued to occupy my mind throughout much of my days and all of my nights.

Of course, I was never as clever as I thought I was. With all of my daily comings and goings, it must have been obvious to Sylvia and other staffers that I wasn't always out of the office on business. I would occasionally be on the receiving end of Sylvia's critical gaze and then throw up a smoke screen of more excuses, justifications, and lies.

Trudi maintained a firm grip on all aspects of our business. She had a keen eye for the details of everything going on inside the office, and if she was aware that I was once again seeing

Catherine, she must have made a choice to live with it for the sake of our two sons whom a divorce would deeply hurt.

But nobody in the office—including Trudi--knew that I had been married to Marilyn, or that I had a sixteen year-old daughter.

Any mail that arrived at The Carey Group was, without exception, business oriented. No personal mail was ever delivered to anyone on the team at the office. Trudi and I each had our desk at opposite ends of a six-by-twelve cubicle, visible to everyone in the open plan office space.

The day I arrived at 9:00 a.m. after an early morning meeting at the city's building department, Trudi was already at her desk. Sylvia's eyes met mine as I walked through the front door, and I immediately knew something was up. She was on her feet, heading me off before I could walk to my desk, handing me an envelope. "This is addressed to you," she said with quiet suspicion.

As quietly as Sylvia had said those words, Trudi's radar was alerted. Before I could sit down at my desk, she looked at me with furrowed brow. "Who's sending you mail at the office?"

I mistakenly believed that my confessions and dramatically abject apologies in our counseling sessions would have calmed Trudi's persistent suspicions. But this time, my answer was uniquely honest. "I don't know," I said as I picked up my letter opener and sliced open the perfectly clean white envelope with my name and our office address neatly written across its face.

As I opened the envelope, a glossy photo of a teenage cheerleader slid out and landed squarely on my desk. My face went cold. I might as well have had "guilty" tattooed across my forehead.

"Who is that?" Trudi asked, now standing over my shoulder, her eyes riveted to the picture lying there in all its full-color glory.

The sound of hurricane-force winds filled my ears. Everything in my sight was suddenly going grey. The colors of my palette were fading, making it impossible to hide the truth. The picture of the boy from Hoboken—the insecure, angry little liar—was bleeding through the layers of dark paint I had always used to disguise my reality.

Trudi knew nothing of my first marriage to Marilyn. It was more than an accidental oversight or a mindless omission. When I met Trudi, when we announced our marriage plans to her family, I said nothing about Marilyn or our baby girl. My failed marriage to Nancy, which ended because of my infatuation with Trudi, was difficult enough to steer past her parents and through our courtship on the way to our marriage. But another marriage—and one that had produced a child—would be beyond the pale and could not be cleverly explained away. And so I had consciously made the strategic decision to simply never mention it.

But now the air was filled with the vibrations of Trudi's suspicions. There was no escaping the avalanche of anger about to come my way.

I slipped the picture back into the envelope and put it in my briefcase. My hands shook as I read the hand-written letter and as Trudi stood there waiting for me to acknowledge her presence. I finished reading the letter, put it in my briefcase, and looked up at her. I cleared my throat, constricted with shame and the certain knowledge of what was to come. "We need to talk. Let's go home."

I walked past Sylvia without saying a word. As I stepped through the door on the way to my car, I heard Trudi snap at Sylvia "We're going home. Call the house if you need us."

I drove along the winding roads through Hope Ranch, passing our country club and the homes of our friends. I saw none of it. My mind was a blur, swirling with confusion, unable to concoct a credible story about the picture or the letter that wouldn't destroy my wife, my children, or the carefully-constructed fiction that was me. I had a solid set of justifications ready to explain it all away, how I only wanted to keep our marriage together, how our two sons would have been hurt, how our careers would have been impacted, how Trudi wouldn't have understood. It was only logical not to reveal my first marriage, given all there was to lose.

The Demon knew all of that, but as I drove toward the beautiful house Trudi and I had built together, I knew it would no longer be my home.

I entered the house first. In my hand I held my briefcase. Inside the briefcase was Tanya's letter. I laid my briefcase on the kitchen counter, opened it, and took it out. I knew Trudi would demand to see it, and that letting her read it would expose my lifetime of deceit.

Trudi entered from the garage, ramrod stiff, expressionless, armored, impenetrable, immune to any more pain.

I followed her to the bedroom so our conversation won't be overheard by our two sons or the housekeeper. Trudi turned to me, saying nothing. She stood there, waiting. Waiting for the truth.

I told her everything.

"I would never have married you, and you know that, if I knew you were divorced twice. Let me see the letter."

I handed it to her and she walked out of the bedroom.

Our marriage was over.

I would never see the letter again.

Tanya: Armor

I waited anxiously as the first week passed.

I was back at school, doing my homework, working out with the cheerleading squad, helping my mother with my brother and sister, trying hard to live a normal teenage life, and the only thing on my mind was what my father would think about my letter, my writing, my picture, me.

A second week came and went.

And another.

Then another.

My heart began to sink.

A full month passed, and I began to recognize the familiar feeling that felt like an anchor repeatedly pulling me under the waters of sorrow and rejection.

There was never going to be a response to my letter. My father was not going to write back to tell me how happy he was that we had finally reconnected, how proud he was of me.

There was only one reality. I wasn't pretty enough, smart enough, or capable enough to be loved and accepted.

He had left me before, left me standing there, waving goodbye to him.

But this was different. I was an insecure sixteen year-old already feeling the sting of yet another rebuff by my biological father. What was wrong with me that I couldn't win my father's approval, time, or even a written response after pouring my soul out to him in a letter? This rejection—after my father had said "Stay in touch"—cut deeply and left a scar that would take decades to heal. It was a scar made of my longing for a real father who would love me unconditionally and protect me from all that was evil. It was a scar that forever chained me to fears of abandonment, neglect, and emotional denial.

The only protection I would ever have would come from the emotional armor I was being forced to build around my heart.

I was the forgotten one, the unclaimed daughter. I would be forever hidden from the light of truth, from the power of love.

I never felt so alone.

Tom: Eulogy

When I heard that my father had passed away, it frightened me.

I now realized that I would never be able to confront him with the truth or get him to acknowledge some shred of responsibility for the life I had lived, for the fear that drove me, for the pain I had inflicted upon those whom I had loved.

We would not reconcile, ever. Any resolution of my many issues with Thomas G. Carey, Sr. could only be made unilaterally.

If I was ever going to come to terms or make peace with my childhood, if I was ever going to understand my insecurities, frustration, and anger, I was on my own. There weren't going to be any apologies or pats on the head or firm handshakes or manly understandings.

At my wife Karen's urging, I had begun writing blog articles about our travels, my art, my feelings. It had been truly cathartic, a way for me to understand the Demon of fear and insecurity passed down to me by my father.

I traveled back to Pennsylvania to be with my mother at his funeral, and I wrote about that trip. There was more to the trip than merely getting my father buried. I wrote so that I could understand:

I knew I would tell my mother of families I've lost, of grandchildren she'll never know. I won't even try to justify the reasons for any of it. Tanya, her first grandchild, is no longer in my life. I'll explain how I justified that and manipulated my own conscience to convince myself Tanya was better off without me, how the divorce from her mother and her move out of California cemented my final separation from my daughter. I'll explain how her two grandsons, my sons, suffered the inevitable destructive consequences of a hidden past forged by my own anger, deceptions, and manipulation.

It will be difficult to tell my mother that I'm a father with a daughter I don't know and two sons who act as though I don't exist.

I'm not sure I'm prepared to hear Mom tell me what sort of son I've been. Will she say I turned away from a dying man and took away my father's last hope for forgiveness? Will I use my evil talent for justification to define my separation from him as a form of personal courage? Or will I tell her about the fear I felt in his household and admit that our estrangement meant I could live life without being afraid of him? Whatever I was going to tell her, it didn't change the fact that I ran away, hid from him, denied my pain and spent decades telling myself a lie: "I'm nothing like my father."

The day of my father's funeral, I sat beside my mother in the church pew. In my hands, I held a copy of his obituary, the story of a man I did not know, but knew too well.

With the reading ability of a severe dyslexic, I decoded the words deliberately, methodically.

My eyes drifted above the paper in my hand. There he was, his face, shoulders, and chest visible in the casket beneath the glass viewing panel. I stared at the plain oak casket, unaffected by the rage, anger, and pain of the past, all now sealed away for eternity.

A delegation of Masons eulogized a man I had never known. They spoke of eternal life after death and the need to perform "good work" toward all humanity throughout the course of a man's life.

Who were they talking about? It certainly wasn't the man lying there in the coffin, not my father.

The Masons were done, their tributes complete. Mother touched my hand and said, "Please say something."

What could I possibly say?

I stood, walked to the casket, and turned to face twenty strangers. My eyes fell on my mother, her sister, and two uncles. Faces of a lost family slowly came into focus. I had traveled thousands of miles to a place I never wanted to see again, for a funeral I would never have attended.

Mom was the only reason I was there. But I found it hard to hold back the anger I had carried for years. I realized my father couldn't threaten or hurt me any longer, but still I wondered: If I say the right thing, will he love me?

For Mom, I found the words. For her, I held back the anger. I spoke to break the echoing silence.

"I haven't been here in a long time. Some of you have spoken of my father as a kind and loving man. Mom, I see the loss in your eyes. I wish I had known the kind and giving man you've lost."

It was the best I could do, the only words I could find. I didn't speak of the embarrassment, humiliation, anger, pain, or fear I felt when I thought of my father.

I walked back to sit beside my mother. She leaned over to me and whispered, "My love for him was lost long ago."

Finally, everyone stood to leave. The Masons, in their tradition, were the last to exit, offering kindness and condolences to those who might need it. Handshakes and hugs were exchanged.

Outside, Mom and I stood alone together for the first time in years. She slipped her arm around my waist and asked "Do you forgive him?"

My answer was silence, the truth catching deep in my throat, forever unspoken:

Forgive my father for the loss of my family, for creating an insecure, frightened child, for the rage inflicted upon my mother, for the warped death threats, for his infidelity and twisted view of sex, for never speaking one word of support or encouragement, for not one memory of kindness in the sixteen years I lived in his house? Forgive a father who pointed only to my failures, who mocked any effort? Forgive a father who said "Get off your lazy ass, quit school, and get a job"? I was fourteen, with a disability

113

and a need for understanding that he saw only as weakness and failure.

No, my father's physical and psychological abuse would never allow me to say "I forgive him." I will only forgive him for passing on to me the short arm of chromosome #6, his only gift to me. That gene mutuation, which made reading so difficult, was the key to my artistic and communication skills. Living with my father taught me that I could use those skills to create beautiful things and that I could get what I wanted by hurting other people.

I will never forgive my father.

Tanya: Taps

Ron and I were married just one month after I graduated high school. Our wedding day was one of high stress and even higher internal anxiety. I couldn't wait to be whisked away by the man who would love me, only me, every hour of every day, forever. I'd waited my entire life to be loved by such a man. Our wedding was attended by a reluctant stepdad who walked me down the aisle in a baby blue tux with a blue ruffled shirt. It really was the style of the day and not just payback. Our parents, friends, and family came to support this painfully shy 18-year-old and her 19-year-old knight in shining armor.

We honeymooned at Cannon Beach on the Oregon coast. We were both exhausted from the long day of nuptials, but when we were in the hotel unpacking, I noticed something odd. "Where's the gun?" I asked.

Ron looked at me curiously, explaining that he didn't bring a gun with him on our honeymoon.

I was incredulous. "What do you mean, you didn't bring a gun?" My tone undoubtedly had an accusatory edge. My Navy SEAL stepfather never went anywhere—not even to the grocery store—without carrying a loaded gun, and I simply couldn't believe that I'd married a man who didn't bring one with him on our wedding day. I cried, thinking this man I had pinned my hopes on to protect me didn't sleep with a gun within reach at all times on his honeymoon. How was this ever going to work?

Ron found himself married to an immature bride with unfulfilled expectations. Like many young marrieds, our home was filled with its share of emotional fireworks, often triggered by feelings of rejection and of being unwanted as a child. Those feelings were packed tightly into my emotional suitcase and hidden away in the attic of my mind, but when I could no longer secure the latches on that aging luggage, we had to consciously work to calm things through prayer and a realization that only God is perfect, even after the emotional fireworks had flown in all their glory.

Our first daughter was born one month to the day after my twentieth birthday. Finally, I had someone who would not leave me, who was not too busy with other things, and into whom I could pour my pent-up torrent of love. Two years later, we were the parents of three little girls.

Life was full and wonderful. Motherhood suited me, and while I worked for a while to help supplement our family finances, my real place, my true calling, was striving to be the best wife and mother I could possibly be.

. . . .

"When reading the Bible one day, it talked about 'honoring your father and mother.' I thought surely that didn't apply to me. And then I sensed the voice I would come to love to hear, that still, quiet whisper that said 'not so fast, Sister.'

"I thought how could God possibly ask me to honor someone that was so dishonorable and had violated my trust? I battled it in my mind that God would surely not expect me to apply this particular passage to my life. But He didn't relent. So I started thinking about how I could honor my stepfather authentically without ignoring the truth of the past. I came to separate the 'position' the Lord had given him in my life for provision. He had a solid work ethic; I could honesty be thankful that I always had food and shelter. God provided that through him. It was the best I could do at the time.

"Several years later, I was watching the news, and it told a story about a man who was going to prison for molesting a girl. I was in my thirties at the time, and I never realized that what had happened to me was illegal. I knew it was wrong, but I thought people only went to prison for rape, and my experience had not been to that degree. But after that one incident, I lived in dread that it might happen again, so I tried to stay in my room and be as invisible as possible. I just tucked that away in my suitcase.

"And a few months later, my dad came to our door. It was strange because he never came to see me after I was married. He had come to ask forgiveness for what he had done. I never felt I held a grudge or resentment. I really didn't feel anything at all, and I wasn't quite sure

116

how to respond. He had just returned from visiting his own ailing father, and something triggered in him the need to make things right. He had risen leaps and bounds over his own upbringing, and had a right to be proud of his accomplishments. I said I forgave him. I felt better, but it didn't make the suitcase disappear. I just put it back up in the attic for safekeeping."

. . . .

September, 1995.

3:00 a.m.

A knock at the door. I opened it to find a friend of my stepfather's standing on our porch, crying. "Tanya, I have something difficult to tell you. Your dad is dead."

I stood there, speechless.

Dennis Winters and my mother had gone through a bitter divorce just a year earlier, and he'd already remarried to a girl my age. Since then, the only contact I'd had with him was an unexpected phone call just three weeks earlier to inform me that he was about to undergo a quadruple cardiac bypass. On that call, for the first time in my life, I thought I'd heard the shadings of fear in his voice. He was fifty years old, and so fit that even his cardiologist had remarked he was the healthiest specimen he'd ever scheduled for this surgery.

My stepfather made it out of the operation with flying colors.

He died in his sleep three days later.

Ron, having an awareness of my history with my stepfather, suggested we go see his body in the hospital. Someone from the family would need to properly identify him and make arrangements for what was to come. Neither my mother nor my siblings were in town that night, leaving only Ron and me to navigate these uncharted waters.

At first, I was reluctant. Ron wrapped me in his arms and assured me it was the right thing to do, that we wouldn't want to have any regrets. I didn't understand what the need to see a dead body had to do with regret, but I trusted that my husband knew something I did not.

We were at the hospital by 3:30 a.m.. A white drape hung from ceiling brackets isolating the body from the rest of the intensive care unit, providing a semblance of privacy for a man who no longer needed it.

117

It was strange, looking at the man who had been my "dad" for more than twenty years, whom I just never connected with. He was strong, confident, unafraid of anything, a hunter and outdoorsman who loved anything to do with adventure, while I was a fearful introvert in fear of my own shadow. He was flat on his back on the hospital gurney, covered only with a paper blanket draped over the full length of his body. Hanging from his right big toe was an off-white card stock tag with his name hand-printed on it. His mouth was open, his chest a swollen barrel. He looked cold. I wanted desperately for someone to bring a blanket for him.

Funeral services for my stepfather were more than awkward. His new wife of one month sat with her family in the front row of benches under dim lighting at the dark-paneled Eagle's Lodge. Across the aisle, my mother Marilyn, my brother and sister, and Ron and I sat together. No cordial acknowledgments from one spouse to another were given. Hatfields & McCoys.

In attendance that day, beyond our small family and a few friends, was the entire roster of the county's deputy sheriffs, each dressed in perfectly-creased uniforms, each wearing a black arm band. Official respect was being paid to one of their own.

For recognition of military service, a flag-folding ceremony was performed. When it was over, the Stars and Stripes was presented to the new wife, now a widow my age. This, after being married to my mother for more than twenty years.

The new widow, who could not give the local newspaper the semblance of an accurate biography to memorialize her husband of one month, was not aware of his military deployments or the fact that he had once been one of the revered, elite snipers of SEAL Team 1.

A graveside bugler played "Taps" and seven uniformed deputies fired a 21-gun salute.

I never shed a tear.

. . . .

"My hope and prayer is that in God's amazing grace, He gave my dad time to make things right before he was ushered to his eternal destiny. My stepdad had his own suitcase. But his dying didn't make my suitcase disappear."

118

Tom: Pinned

Karen and I sat in bed as I listened to the voice of a woman I didn't know, but who knew me all too well.

I moved my legs beneath the sheets, a barely discernable move to disguise my anxiety. My palms were suddenly moist and my stomach began to tighten.

I knew why Karen wanted me to listen to this unknown woman. Her voice was gentle, tinged with shades of sadness and regret, artfully veiled with a confidence earned over the years of her life. She had painted over harsh colors with her own broad brush. Where mine was a brush of deceit and emotional forgery, hers was a brush of forgiveness.

Before I met Karen and was forced to understand myself, I would have done more than shuffle around in the sheets. I would have run away, avoided the pain, hidden from the truth.

But here was the truth, spoken by Tanya in her oral testimony before a church congregation. The pain of her words was going to be mine to bear.

I turned to Karen. "She seems nervous. Yet her voice is calm. Is this who I think it is?"

The voice grew more confident, more powerful, and I was drawn to it.

"As the light went on in the attic, I saw my Mom married when she was seventeen, her senior year in high school. Her new husband had to sign her report cards. After she graduated, he moved her to New York where his family lived. When she got pregnant with me, her best friend, who happened to also be her cousin, came to New York to be with my mom..."

119

I looked at Karen. My heart skipped several major beats, nearly coming out of my chest. "Is this Tanya?"

"Listen, just listen."

I did. I listened to my only daughter.

"My dad got her pregnant too…so somewhere in this world I have a half brother who is also a cousin. He was also messing around with his college professor. (Talk about a soap opera). My dad was also very abusive, as well as an avid adulterer. After I was born, he pushed my mom and me down a flight of stairs. Mom finally decided to leave him. One day I was living with a mommy and daddy, the next day I didn't have a daddy anymore. There would be no birthday cards, no Christmas cards, no calls or contact of any kind. Along with packing my favorite life-sized doll with the pink floppy hat, I also packed with me that day the shoes of abandonment in the suitcase of my mind."

Karen gave me a look that stopped me cold. I was a butterfly pinned to a cork board. Escape was not possible. "I can't believe what I'm hearing. There's more to this story than this," I said.

Her face was calm, placid. "Just listen," Karen said.

I did. The voice cracked, tearful, courageous.

"My mom took me back to Southern California, and she married again, and that marriage was annulled. Then she and another man tried to rent the same apartment on the beach in Coronado. She won. But he got the apartment next door. One day she left a paper grocery bag on the stove burner, he found it and saved the day. Apparently, that was enough grounds to get married again."

My mind was racing as I tried to piece this story together. My stomach knotted and tears began to well in my eyes. There was no turning back now.

Karen was crying as she watched tears run down my face. I knew as I listened to this voice that I was listening to the life story of my daughter, Tanya. "I need to know what happened to her!" I said.

120

Karen, who had never had the opportunity to be a mother, couldn't understand how I could ever abandon a child, and she began asking me questions.

"I'll answer all your questions," I said, "but just let me listen to the rest of this and then we'll talk."

Tears of sorrow filled Karen's eyes while tears of guilt, embarrassment, and regret filled mine as I listened to every last word.

"My life went on, but every once in awhile something would trigger in my spirit, like an uninvited guest, and I would want to go and rummage through the suitcase to see if the clothes still fit – they always did. I was trying to find a way I could forgive authentically without dismissing the reality of what had occurred.

"It was when I truly connected with what Jesus said on the cross, 'Father forgive them for they don't know what they do.' So I applied that to my situation...Father forgive my dad, he had no idea that a few moments of self- gratification would cause lifelong imprints of insecurity and feelings of having no value. That a few moments would affect my future husband for years to come because I had a warped view of sexuality. That it would affect how I relate to men in general.

"I applied the same principle to my biological dad. Father forgive my dad, for he had no idea that abandoning and rejecting his daughter would have lingering effects of insecurity and internal battles of not being wanted or loved.

"How do I know for sure that I have forgiven them? Because it is one of my heart's great desires to have my dad greet me at the gates of heaven. I pray for my biological dad and his family also that they would come to know and receive this incredible gift that God has so generously bestowed on me. His new family doesn't know about us. He's carrying a lot of baggage in his own suitcase of life."

Karen and I sat there, staring at her iPad.

"Are you going to call Tanya?" she asked.

I tried to see through hot tears, my throat so tight it hurt. "I want to call."

I sat on the bed quietly, my mind a blur as I tried to make sense of everything we'd just heard. I was trying to imagine how

Tanya would feel if I called. I wasn't sure I had the courage to call her.

It had been uncomfortable, embarrassing, and painful to listen to Tanya's memories of me. Now I had to process all of this, to give it some thought. I'm not an impulsive person, given to acting without knowing all the facts. I needed to evaluate all of what we'd just heard and carefully consider next moves, if there were any to make. I had spent years avoiding truth, omitting details, deflecting responsibility; this was as good an opportunity as any to let this be someone else's decision.

I looked to Karen. "I don't want to intrude on Tanya's life if it causes any problems for her. She seems to be in a good place and opening old wounds may, as she says, require a trip to her baggage in the attic." Perfectly rational, as always. Avoiding the issue, as always. Karen had me frozen in her high beams. I relented. "I think I should call her husband. He'll know if Tanya will talk to me."

I was being evasive and cowardly, and I was scared to death.

The chill never left our bedroom that night. Sleep would be slow in coming.

Tanya: Gloria

Two weeks after my stepfather's funeral, our phone rang and I picked it up. The woman on the other end of the call introduced herself as "Gloria," and announced that she was my maternal grandmother.

I didn't remember her or even recognize her name.

She explained that she was the mother of my biological father, Tom Carey, Jr.

I stood there, the phone in my hand, silent. I had no idea of how I should respond. I asked her how she had acquired my phone number, and she explained that my mother, Marilyn, had called her.

Without telling me about any of this, my mother apparently felt it would be "a good idea" for me—at age 30—to connect with my biological family.

Gloria tentatively began sharing a little about herself and her daughter who lived with her, never mentioning my dad. It was an awkward conversation and totally unexpected as she continued to tell me where she lived, whom she lived with, the fact that her husband had recently passed away close to the time my stepfather had died, and how she was suffering from diabetes.

I listened intently, trying to make sense of this call from an unknown woman claiming to be my grandmother, and then she asked me "How tall are you?"

I told her, and quickly learned how proud she was that her late husband and her son were both well over six feet tall, a gene that apparently skipped the women in our bloodline.

During this conversation, which felt quite awkward to me at this point in my life, she mentioned my three daughters. Apparently my mother had told this woman more than my phone number. We spoke for another few minutes, and she asked if she could correspond with me by mail. Not knowing what to say, I agreed, and we ended our little chat.

After that, she wrote a couple of times, but I had three girls in school, each with a full schedule of activities and social engagements, and I didn't have space or time in my life to establish a relationship with Gloria, a complete stranger who lived on the other side of the country. In one of her letters she did mention that my father had two sons who were my daughter's ages, and questions flashed across my mind: Was he a "present dad" to his sons? Was I still a secret from his past that his family knew nothing about?

Tom: Morning

A s expected, it had been a long, restless night with sleep nothing more than an elusive mirage.

I awakened early, with Tanya's testimonial echoing in my mind. Karen slept beside me as I considered my options. I could call. Or not. It might be best if I wrote a letter.

I slid out of bed, trying not to awaken Karen. As quietly as possible, I went downstairs to our home office. I wanted to reread several chapters of "Dyslexia: A Good and Evil Gift," the memoir I'd been writing about my life with a disability, while Tanya's words were still fresh in my mind. I suspected that my dyslexia was at the root of the way I had conducted my life. I had to find something to blame besides myself, and I needed some quiet moments of alone before Karen came downstairs with her questions about the things Tanya had said.

I had just sat down when I heard Karen coming down from the bedroom, so I met her at the bottom of the stairs. "We should talk," I said.

"I need a cup of coffee." Her eyes were red and swollen and I know she saw the sadness in mine.

We got our coffee and sat on the couch and I asked her how she even found Tanya's testimonial.

She said she had found my father's obituary online, and it noted his granddaughter-in-law Tanya and his great-grandchildren Lindsi, Kali, and Misti, three names uniquely ending in the same letter. "I realized that when I told you about the obituary, you had no idea you had grandchildren. I thought putting you in touch with Tanya might resolve some of the guilt you've been carrying around for leaving her." Then Karen revealed just how much of an internet detective she is. "I searched all four of their names together and Tanya's husband's name appeared with the name of his church."

I was blown away. Who would ever have figured all that out? My brilliant, loving wife, that's who.

"When I found the church's website I found Tanya's name linked to an audio file of a recently posted testimonial. Then I just downloaded the voice clip," she said. "I listened to it several times and knew you needed to hear what she had to say. She said she forgave you."

I sat there in stunned silence.

"She needs to hear you apologize, Tom. She needs to hear you say you're sorry for leaving. That's why I wanted you to hear it."

I was still marooned in my own ego, my narcissistic self-preservation. "I don't think Tanya will want to talk to me. I had a chance to reconnect with her when she was sixteen, and I screwed that up." A dose of *mea culpa* was my out, the perfect dodge.

Karen looked at me. The caffeine had kicked in and she meant business. "I don't care what happened when she was sixteen. You need to call her," she said.

My back was against the wall. "I need to listen to it again to make sure you're right," I said.

I knew Karen had questions, but she didn't ask them. I downloaded Tanya's audio file to my computer and listened to her testimonial again.

I heard the daughter whom I had neither seen nor spoken to in more than thirty years, and I felt an immediate connection. The metaphoric suitcase in her attic was not closed. I needed to talk to her so she could either empty it or seal it shut forever. I also felt I needed to clarify some of the facts of the story she had told.

"I don't want to create any problems for Tanya," I said. "She's found strength in her faith. As she herself said, 'the light is on in the attic now' and her faith will guide her if she decides to open that suitcase. That's why I'm hesitant to call."

Because Tanya was married to a Christian pastor, I hoped he could apply his skills as a minister to find out if she wanted to

126

talk to me. I thought I could surreptitiously contact him without imposing on Tanya directly. Still, I hesitated. I looked to Karen with no uncertain anxiety. "Are you sure this is a good idea?" I asked.

Without a moment of hesitation, she said "Call."

I dialed the church's number.

"Wellspring Bible Fellowship," a woman said.

I stumbled. What if they asked why I was calling? Who did I want to talk to? Am I making this call for me or for Tanya?

"Can I help you?" rang in my ear.

"I'd like to speak to the pastor, please," I said.

"He's not in."

I felt the air rush out of my lungs. A reprieve. I could leave a message and not deal with my fear of rejection. I wouldn't have to hear anyone tell me that my daughter didn't want to talk to me. My stress was gone. I went into Professional Tom Mode. "Please let the pastor know Thomas Carey from Santa Barbara called," I said, and left my return number.

"Is there any message?"

"He'll know." It was the only answer I could think of.

"Okay. He'll be in tomorrow. I'll let him know you called."

I hung up the phone, looked to Karen as though I had just scaled Everest. "I did it. Let's see what happens."

That night, I went to my desk and wrote about my father's funeral. I was the son who could not forgive his father, yet I had just heard the voice of my daughter forgiving me.

Tom G. Carey & Tanya Laeger

Tanya: Messages

After sharing my story at our church, the emotional toll was profound and unexpected. Had I dishonored my fathers by sharing my story? Did I share too much? I was grateful that we had previously planned a trip to Colorado. I was ready for a vacation, so we took a trip to to visit our youngest daughter.

The day we returned from our trip, Ron asked me to step into his office to go through all the messages he'd received while we were gone. There on his desk were a dozen or more sticky-notes and phone message slips.

Out of the myriad of pink messages, my eyes immediately landed on the name: Thomas Carey. I thought it was pretty strange for someone with my father's name to call the church to ask for financial help of some kind, which had become a fairly common occurrence when people were in dire straits. I had become frustrated with people who would never set foot in church to attend a service, but who didn't mind coming in to ask for money. So seeing that name—my father's name—on that slip of paper perplexed me.

But Ron was already way ahead of me. The return number included a California area code, and he thought it might be my biological father. "I wonder if he needs a kidney?" Ron queried. I immediately started thinking about what I would do if he actually did need a kidney.

Ron asked if I was okay with him returning the call to see what this man wanted. I thought that by sharing my story, I had closure, that I would never see or hear from my biological father again. I was completely at peace with that.

So why was his name coming back into my life now?

I went home and waited.

Tom: October

Octtober days are generally balmy and pleasant in Santa Barbara, each one passing more quickly than the previous with the approach of winter. But this October day passed slowly. Too slowly.

I'd been up late the night before, writing about my father's funeral, and loose thoughts of him were still rattling around in my mind.

But the thoughts that weighed heaviest on me were those of Tanya. I wondered what she would think if she knew I couldn't forgive my own father.

In our small home office, Karen sits no more than three feet away from me. Ever alert, when she heard my cell phone ring she quickly asked "Who is it?"

I looked at the phone's screen. "It's from Oregon."

She didn't hesitate or allow me to. "Answer it."

I always answer with "Hi, this is Tom."

The voice on the other end was unfamiliar, the voice of the son-in-law I had yet to meet. "Is this Thomas Carey?"

"Yes."

"This is Ron Laeger." All business.

"Hi, Ron. Do you know who I am?"

"Yes," he said. "I know who you are. What can I do for you?"

He had a way of getting to the point, so I took his cue. "I heard Tanya's testimonial and wanted to ask you if she would be willing to talk to me." Silence. He was listening, waiting for more, so I continued. "I don't want to impose on her or cause any problems. That's why I wanted to talk to you first." More silence, more listening. I took a hopeful breath and tried to wrap it up as quickly as possible, not wanting to sound obnoxious about any of this. "It seemed to me, after listening to her testimonial, that she may want to talk. And I would love to talk to her."

That was it, my entire pitch. I had been nothing but a memory for her over the past thirty years. I was now the phantom father offering to come back into her life. I knew how presumptuous it must have sounded on the other end of the call.

"I'll have to ask her when I get home tonight. I'm sure she'll want to think about it," he said. "Can I call or text you if she decides to talk to you?" Calm, to the point, without judgment, with neither promise nor rejection. I could sense an understanding wisdom in his voice. No wonder he was a pastor.

And then the call was over. I looked at my phone, feeling as though it held the answer. But there was none. Ron had committed to nothing, and while I felt a sense of great relief at having reached out, I felt suddenly vulnerable. What if he never calls back? What if Tanya wants nothing to do with me?

My insecurities fluttered, but I couldn't let the Demon rear his narcissistic head. It was too late now to quickly find my palette of lies and manipulation, too late to brush the colors of deceit over the canvas of a life Karen had helped me lay bare, a life where I had come to believe that honesty and love are the only values of any worth.

Karen looked me squarely in the eye, her natural bottom-line instincts burning through me. "Tell me exactly what he said."

"He was at work and said he would ask Tanya when he went home if she would be comfortable with a call from me."

"And?" Karen doesn't share my patient approach to things, preferring immediate answers and immediate solutions.

"He didn't commit to her calling. He said she would more than likely have to think about it. So we wait and see." That was all there was, nothing more. I knew it wouldn't be enough for Karen. She had serious questions for me, questions it was now time to ask.

"Did you push Tanya and her mother down a flight of stairs?" She looked at me, unblinking, watching my reaction, gauging my current commitment to the truth in our marriage, to the truth of my past, to the truth of who I had been and who I had, over the past fifteen years, become.

"That's a difficult question to answer with just a yes or no," I said. "I've written in my blog about leaving Tanya and her mother."

But I'd never written anything or mentioned anything to Karen about pushing Tanya and her mother down the stairs. Now I told her everything I remembered about my breakup with Marilyn, about my going to the community college and my affair with Marilyn's cousin. I recited my long list of justifications for a life of unjustifiable behavior and volunteered a broad spectrum of details about how and why I'd manipulated the truth at ever turn in my life, all to protect the insecure little boy from Hoboken. None of it answered Karen's question, so she asked it again.

"What does all this have to do with you pushing Tanya and her mother down the stairs?"

After more than forty years, the answer was difficult to put into words. When I was done telling Karen what I personally recalled about that day, the details of which varied somewhat from what we'd heard in Tanya's testimonial, I looked into Karen's eyes. "There is no excuse for what happened, I've had to live with this and many other bad decisions in my life. This is a part of my story I've never been able to tell."

But hearing Tanya tell that story, it had all come back. The pain and remorse of what I'd done had been pushed into the recesses of my mind, and now they were here, in the present, covering me like a rash. I had to deal with it or it would eat me alive.

And so I had begun writing my story as the only way for me to understand the Demon and to accept the fact that the Demon was me.

It had been a long, emotionally draining day. Long ago, Karen and I had made a commitment to talk about everything and anything, no matter how difficult it might be. I had confessed everything to Karen, fully exposing the darkest parts of my past.

Karen sat there listening to me tell it all. "I believe I've changed," I said to her. "The more I write about my past, the more I understand what an asshole I've been. If Tanya can forgive me, then I have to accept responsibility for everything I've done. I can't change the past, but I can be honest about it."

Night was approaching as the October day faded into a glowing orange sunset.

It would be another sleepless night, but tonight we would sleep in each other's arms. The chill had left the room.

· · · ·

October 14, 2011.

We awakened early and began our day with the usual morning coffee. We checked our email. I did some writing. Karen researched online details for our next vacation.

My phone lay on the desk next to my keyboard. Suddenly, it vibrated. I looked at the phone and the text from Ron: "Tanya wants to talk to you. She'll be home all day."

My mouth went dry as my eyes filled and then overflowed.

I couldn't speak. I just held my phone up for Karen to see, so she could read the text herself.

Through my tears I looked at my wife and whispered, "Thank you."

Tanya: Plans

I left Ron's office and went home, not really knowing what to think or what to expect. I waited for his call.

I fought to keep my emotions in check, to preserve the protective armor that had for so long shielded the heart of this little girl now living in the body of an adult. I thought I had just closed this chapter in my life and was totally unprepared for a sequel.

The phone rang and a deep voice echoed in my ear for the first time in over 30 years. "Hello Tanya, this is your father."

I didn't know what to say, but having learned to keep careful command of my emotions, I just listened to the stranger on the phone who called himself my father. He shared that he had discovered and listened online to the story—which I had no idea was being recorded at the time—I had made at our church just weeks earlier, the principal subject of which was *forgiving my father!*

He said he was sorry for what he had done and for what he had not done, and that he was no longer the man who had hurt me twice before. He shared many details of his life now: he had retired from architecture, was devoted to self-examination, writing, painting and golf. He talked about taking a writing class so that he could process his past life by writing his memoirs. He'd even started his own online blog, sharing his thoughts, writings and paintings.

I listened carefully, taking in every word. He asked me if we could continue to correspond via email. I was reticent, not sure my heart could take another promise made and not kept, another rejection. Now that I felt I had closed that chapter, I wasn't sure if I was ready to walk back into a room that echoed with past hurt and rejection. However, email seemed safe enough. The digital distance would give me time to process his words and reply thoughtfully, at my own pace and in my own time.

As soon as we hung up, I went to the computer and looked up his blog.

The first words I read were, "I'll never forgive my father." I soon became engrossed in reading a story that began with his childhood and ended at the grave of his own father. I was mesmerized by every word, taking in every detail, but I also noted interesting spelling and grammatical errors that did nothing to hide an amazing ability to write with profound creativity, thought and insight. My father was able to express his unique emotional vocabulary in an extraordinary way.

He was obviously a very gifted writer and painter. I soon learned that he had dyslexia but that he didn't find out until he was in his fifties. Reading about his own insecurities and fears from his childhood, along with the discovery of his dyslexia and how it had affected him growing up, and how he had learned to compensate all those years without knowing it, helped me to understand the man, my father, in a very different light. No longer did I see the stern father filled with anger who left his blonde, pigtailed three-year-old little girl standing in the front yard all those years ago. Now I saw a man in the fullness and complexity of our shared human condition, with fears and insecurities just like my own.

In exchanging periodic emails over the next several months, I discovered that my father and I are similar in so many ways and very different in others.

I had always turned to God to find peace and fulfillment, to make sense of our world and to find my place and purpose in it. My father is agnostic, with no real belief or faith in God.

I'm a simple girl, still loving the comfort, routine and security of home and family life. My father is an accomplished architect, painter, writer and world traveler. He and his wife live in sun-drenched California, while my husband and I live in the Land-of-a-Hundred-Valleys in Oregon. We're both introspective and thoughtful. We both have an intrinsic creative side expressed in a shared love of writing; thus, the writing and compilation of this book.

Was discovering my father a random accident made possible through his accidental discovery of my testimony? Was forgiving my father the key to moving forward in my own life?

I believe that God has a plan for each of us, and He works that plan every day. He had been working overtime for me.

Tom: Images

A church, technology, and the internet opened the door for Tanya and me to overcome time and distance, allowing us reconnect.

I've always enjoyed and embraced technological change. My earliest memory of a quantum shift in technology was when our Emerson tube radio was replaced with a 1948 Motorola television. Fifty years later, this dyslectic's dream, a desktop computer, was on my office desk. Along with the glowing monitor and flat keyboard—a major novelty compared to our office typewriters—came software that would correct spelling. I could write without appearing dyslexic. Today's technology is the stuff of childhood sci-fi dreams; now I'm about to talk face-to-face to Tanya over the internet via Skype.

After several phone calls and e-mails, Tanya and I planned to see and speak to each other online. It was an exciting thought, seeing the girl I'd left behind nearly forty years ago. Karen and I sat in our Santa Barbara living room, waiting to see and hear my daughter and her husband.

Karen staged things, wanting to make a good impression. We sat in front of a flickering fireplace in a room where historic paintings hung as a back drop for contemporary furnishings. Our post-and-beam home is a French bungalow cottage perched on a hillside. Ally, our Pomeranian, sat on Karen's lap. Placed on a side table in view of the iPad camera was the photograph of Tanya in her cheerleading uniform she had mailed to me when she was just sixteen.

One or two taps on the screen and our iPad snapped to life with the image of my daughter. A beautiful, grown woman. I was looking at my daughter for the first time in over thirty years. Tanya was sitting next to Ron in their Roseburg, Oregon, home.

The visual component of communication added an unspoken reserve to the conversation. The new medium revealed hidden, uncomfortable stresses in our eyes and on our faces. The conversation moved from "You are beautiful," to "Your home is charming," to "I can't believe how clearly we can see each other as we speak."

The stumbling small talk came to an abrupt end when Tanya suddenly invited Karen and me to visit her and Ron over the forthcoming Christmas Holiday.

It would be a Christmas to remember.

Tanya: Fumbling

The picture popped up on our iPad screen and there sat a silver-haired man, handsome and proper, with his beautiful wife beside him. Light from a fireplace illuminated a picturesque and charming living room filled with warmth.

My biological father was still quite unfamiliar. We had been emailing for a month or so, but now we were looking at each other. We had agreed this would be the next step in our relational journey.

Ron sat beside me as I greeted the handsome man and his wife. A few minutes into the conversation, I noticed on the table a picture of a young girl in a cheerleading outfit. It was the photo I had sent him more than thirty years ago.

We all fumbled through a somewhat awkward conversation, but agreed to continue communicating. Before our Skype session, my oldest daughter had suggested an invitation to our family Christmas so we could meet personally. I knew that my father had never seen his three beautiful granddaughters or his great grandchildren. In fact, he had been a bit startled to learn he was, in fact, a great-grandfather.

As the four of us sat there staring at each other over the internet connection, I nervously invited my father and his wife to join us in Roseburg for Christmas. With the holiday only two months away, I was certain they would already have plans, but they immediately accepted the invitation.

The pressure was on.

Excitement, anticipation, and stress surged through our household. All of a sudden, there was a need to have the house in tip-top shape and the Christmas stockings hung on the mantel for all the family. (Something I had wanted to do for years but never got around to doing).

What names should I put on their stockings? At first, we had called them Tom and Karen, but we wanted to make them feel part of the family when they walked into our home for the very first time. We settled on "Dad and Mumsy." As I applied those names to their new stockings and hung them above our fireplace, it looked strange. It had been so long since I had called anyone "Dad."

We already knew Karen had a great sense of humor. Our three daughters and their families were going to come and meet their new grandfather. A sense of excitement and anticipation filled the air. Each of our daughters had already emailed their grandfather and his wife and introduced themselves. It was an odd feeling, seeing how openly our daughters showed such acceptance and love for this man, a grandfather, whom they had never known and whom they'd never met.

Then came the biggest dilemma of all: what does one give an estranged father for a first Christmas gift after the passage of thirty years? What is even appropriate? Somehow the usual sweater or cologne didn't seem to fit the bill. This would take some thought as gift-giving is not one of my primary love languages.

The day finally arrived. The house was sparkling clean with a fresh candle signifying the light of hope that filled the air. Stockings had been hung with care, and nerves were all a-twitter.

While we waited for their arrival, Karen was giving us text-message updates as they travelled the I-5 Corridor from Santa Barbara to Oregon. Ron and I puttered around the house to work off nervous energy, re-cleaning the kitchen sink and replacing the pillows on the couch, and then we heard their car pull up in front of our driveway.

We walked outside on that cold December afternoon, overcome with emotion. I hugged my father for the first time in more than three decades. I hadn't seen his face for over half my life. Tears flowed on both sides.

It is said that our lives are not lived in days but in moments. This was a moment that would be treasured, a moment of new beginnings.

Tom: Journey

Tanya had seen my canvas stripped. I had publicly exposed all the shameful, hurtful, self-serving details of my life on my blog and in the chapters of my memoir. She had read all about the ugly images I had worked so hard to conceal on the canvas of my life.

Her ability to forgive me touched me to the core. I felt the warmth of freshly-applied colors now. My canvas had changed. Tanya saw those changes and recognized that I had changed.

We accepted Tanya's invitation. We would drive to Oregon to celebrate Christmas with my daughter, her husband, my granddaughters, and great-grandchildren. A family unknown to me just one month ago.

Preparations and travel plans were made. We then focused on gifts. What would be appropriate for us to give to my newly rediscovered family?

The great-grandchildren were easy. A phone call to Lindsi, my oldest granddaughter, who had excellent advice. We agreed it would be an American Girl baby doll for Lilly. Judah, my youngest great-grandchild, loved trucks, so a construction set with trucks would be his first gift from great-grandparents he would meet for the first time.

My granddaughters Lindsi, Kali, and Misti were next on Santa's list. I had talked to each of them on the phone and e-mailed them as Tanya showed her trust by allowing me to contact the girls. In conversations with each granddaughter, I learned that they appreciated and enjoyed my sketches from Europe, which I had posted online. I found a sketch I felt reflected the interest of each of the girls and they were wrapped with great apprehension and anticipation.

But what would I give Tanya?

The tagline to my online blog reads "Writing and art as I see it and write it." One of the sections of my blog displays my artwork. Tanya had told me she loved one particular painting I had posted. She spoke of a strong connection to the watercolor I called "A Castle on the Danube." My sketches and paintings have always been an expression of my deepest feelings. This painting would be a very personal gift for Tanya.

I had heard Tanya's story of the pain I'd repeatedly caused in her life. I now wanted the thought behind our gifts to somehow convey my heartfelt wish for a new future free of pain, filled with compassion, caring, and love.

We left Santa Barbara on December 11th and headed north. It would be a two-day drive with an overnight stop in Napa Valley. As we drove along, Karen and I were quiet. The radio played Christmas carols. Open fields and vineyards flew by outside. We each anticipated the moment Tanya and I would stand face to face.

Suddenly, out of nowhere, Karen blurted out, "Can you believe it?" Then an extended moment of silence was followed by "You're going to meet your daughter!"

All I was thinking about was a little girl in pigtails.

I tracked our 764- mile trip from Napa to Roseburg on my phone. As we drove, I watched the miles melt away, fewer than one hundred miles to go.

We watched Mount Shasta rise from the valley floor as we ticked off the miles to Roseburg. Twenty miles to go, I was in a fog of anticipation as Karen texted and called Ron for directions. "Can you believe it?" rang repeatedly through the car.

My mind was spinning: what do I say, should I hug her, will I cry, what will she say, will she cry?

I saw the miles go from one to zero on my phone as we pulled to the curb in front of the address we'd been given. "Is this the house?" I asked. I fumbled with my phone, subconsciously stalling, hesitant to get out of the car.

Karen and Ally jumped out instinctively. Ally ran to a neighbor walking her dog. Karen gave chase and asked the dog walker to confirm the address she had on her phone.

142

The door of the house we had parked in front of opened. Ron and Tanya appeared. She was tiny, with blond hair and sky-blue eyes. There are no words to describe what happened next. We walked to each other and hugged for what seemed eternity. I cried, Tanya cried, Ron cried, Karen cried and Ally – well, if a dog could cry - she cried as well. The tears were warm, kind tears held for thirty-three years.

A father and daughter reunited.

Our welcome was genuine and caring, with a touch of reserve, a DNA trait Tanya and I share. "Reserved" is not a Ron or Karen characteristic. They became quick friends and shared stories that Tanya and I would need much more time to share.

Tanya prepared dinner and reported that Misti, my granddaughter, would stop by soon. The youngest child and last to leave home, Misti was the first to come home for the Christmas holiday, and was anxious to meet this new family she had only recently heard about.

Karen had prepared a PowerPoint presentation for my sixtieth birthday, documenting my journey through life, and she had brought it along to share with Ron and Tanya.

Karen and Ron worked out some technical difficulties with equipment and my life soon flashed by on the large-screen TV in Tanya's living room. As we endured what seemed to be an endless and personally embarrassing presentation of my professional accomplishments as produced by my biggest fan in life, Karen, we managed to ignore the elephant in the room: that I had abandoned Tanya more than once.

Misti had been visiting in-laws, and when she walked through the door Tanya appeared at her side, the instinctively protective mother. Tanya pointed in my direction with "This is your grandfather, Tom."

I watched the large, blue eyes Misti shared with her mother well up. Without hesitation she approached and hugged me so tight that it took my breath away. Tears of joy, tears for her mother's happiness. The sensitive, creative child of my child is stunningly beautiful and embodies her mother's creativity and her father's sense of adventure.

Things began to blur. Emotions flowed as a river.

I was in my daughter's home, comfortable and surprised at how secure I felt surrounded by all the Christmas cheer. The front door opened again with the arrival of Lindsi, her husband Josh, and my great-grandchildren, Lilly and Judah. Kali lived some distance away, and I wouldn't be able to meet her until the following day, but this would truly be a Christmas Eve to remember. I sat in silence as I saw the joy in the children's faces. They tore into their wrapped presents with the enthusiasm we only know as children.

Lilly was shy, with familiar sky-colored eyes. She opened her gifts delicately and with precision. Judah needed a little help from his dad to remove the colorful paper; each gift held his attention a short time before he moved on.

After the children opened their presents, it was play time with their new-found treasures.

As the children played, Tanya and Ron passed out the gifts remaining under the tree. Lindsi was the first to open hers—a pen-and-ink sketch I had made while in Italy—and with a warm thank you said, "Your sketch will always remind me that one day Mom and I will travel to Italy." Misti opened her gift and recognized my sketch of the Opera house in Vienna. She told me her sketch would always remind her of her visit to Vienna and how much she loved to travel. I saw my granddaughter's

144

appreciation and knew they understood the thought Karen and I had given to each of their gifts.

Ron handed Tanya the gift I'd brought for her. She unwrapped it carefully, apprehensively. As she unwrapped my watercolor painting "Castle Along the Danube," the glass in the frame reflected her tears. Her eyes told me that the true message of my gift, *I'm so sorry. Thank you for bringing me into your family, thank you for seeing I've changed and, most of all, thank you for your forgiveness,* had found its way into her heart.

There was nothing more I could ever have hoped for. This was a magical Christmas.

I sat on the hearth, my back warmed by the fire. My head brushed the stocking, hung by Tanya with the letters "D – A – D" embroidered on it. When Ron handed me a beautifully wrapped gift—this one from Tanya—I was overwhelmed. I slowly removed the Christmas paper and saw a glass covered three-paneled picture frame. In each frame, on parchment-colored paper, a story was told. Under the printed words in the first panel was the faint image of a pirate. Beneath the words in the second panel was the image of a child's hands. Under the last panel of the story was the photo of Tanya and me as we hugged on the first day we arrived in Roseburg.

I was speechless as I read her story, "The Prince and His Search for Treasure."

Tanya: Treasure

We welcomed my father and Karen into our home, and after giving them a short tour through the house, we sat down at our dining room table under the soft light from the chandelier and started talking. The words were coming easier now. We talked about the people and places we each remembered; some things we both recalled, some things we didn't. It was an evening filled with remembrances and discovery.

One by one, our daughters—all in their twenties now—arrived. They were immediately choked up as they hugged their grandfather for the first time in their entire lives. My father gazed into the eyes of his grandchildren and great-grandchildren for the first time. He saw his legacy in the reflection of the two youngest who would continue to carry his DNA.

It was a night filled with emotion, lively conversation, and plenty of cautious curiosity.

On Christmas Eve, our entire family attended the candlelight service featuring the children's choir singing with their angelic voices. It is our tradition to open gifts on Christmas Eve, and I wanted to give my father his gift after everyone else had received all of theirs. His would be the last one opened. There were plenty of the usual joys and squeals from the kids as they opened their gifts and the sweet thank you's for other meaningful exchanges.

Then my father presented me with a large, rectangular gift. Inside was an exquisite hand-painted watercolor he called "Castle Along the Danube." This painting in particular stood out among all the other spectacular pieces he had posted on his blog. It was breathtaking and touched me deeply. It was the first thing given from his hand, a part of himself, portrayed in the image of the castle. The shading lingered along the castle walls, reflected in the river below. It wasn't just the castle reflected in the waters, but the man himself.

Finally, it was my turn to give my father his present. I was so excited to give it to him; I could hardly wait until all the other gifts had been exchanged. With our family gathered all around, I handed my father his gift. He opened it slowly as he sat in front of the fireplace where his Christmas stocking draped gently behind him with glittering letters spelling out "Dad."

Ironically, my gift mirrored the theme of the castle painting I had just received, because in every fairy tale a castle needs a prince.

As he carefully unwrapped the iridescent Christmas wrapping, a framed picture of a creative short story I had written about him was revealed. I had taken all the information I had gleaned from his blog and his online memoir and distilled in writing what his words had revealed to me. I called it "The Prince and His Search for Treasure."

• • • •

The Prince and His Search for Treasure

Once upon a time in a land far, far away, a young prince was born. His beautiful mother loved him very much, but his father was a very harsh and troubled king. As the young prince grew up into a handsome young boy, the longing of his tender little heart yearned to hear the words... "this is my son, whom I love, in him I am well pleased."

But alas, the young lad was never to hear the expressions of love and affirmation from the man he wanted most in the world to please. And after a time, he stopped fighting the battle he knew he could not win.

So when the young prince turned sixteen, he boarded a ship called the U.S.S. Cambria and sailed to distant lands. He took two treasures with him on that fate-filled day. One was a locked treasure box he kept hidden deep under his breast-shield of shiny armor, of which he never took off, even when he slept. On his voyages, he would look for the key that would unlock the box and reveal the treasure hidden deep within.

The second treasure was a brilliant double-edged sword. The upper side of the sword was called "anger," the underside of the sword was called "pain." This special sword was forged in the flames of suffering, hurt, inner turmoil, insecurity and rejection. He wielded this sword with mastery as he fought off the dragons, both within and without.

The young prince grew into a handsome man and as such he met and married beautiful maidens, but alas, he was ever the warrior, yielding the double-edged sword of "anger" and "pain" wherever he went. No one knew this was done to keep the other treasure hidden beneath the armor made of steel untouched. He had yet to find the special key that would unlock the box to reveal the treasure buried within. His search would continue.

Then one day the handsome prince had a baby daughter. But because he had yet to discover the key to his treasure box, he had to continue his search, fighting the dragons, both within and without. Two more sons were born to the prince, and still, the ever-present search to find the illusive key overshadowed his ability to fully rest in the love and relationships that were his for the asking.

Many years and many voyages have passed, and now, in a season of reflection, the prince has laid down his sword only to discover the sword did not protect his first treasure, it was a pathway to it. The prince removed his ever-present armor as he discovered the long-illusive key to the treasure box. It was called the "key of forgiveness." It unlocked the treasure box that hindered his tender heart, the one that was put away in the treasure box as a tender young boy. Now his greatest treasure, his heart, was free to live and love in light of that forgiveness. And at long last he can hear the words he has longed to hear, not from his father, but from his daughter. . .

You are my father, Whom I love,
In you, I am well pleased.
With all my heart in my treasure box,   Tanya Marie

• • • •

My father read the story attentively, and I saw tears in his eyes. I wondered how he interpreted a story I'd written, gleaned from my reading about his life.

There we sat, both with the first gifts given to each other in over three decades. Heart-filled representations of the canvas of the heart that had been locked away, deep in storage, now exposed to the light and made more valuable with the passage of many years.

Emotions revealed what mere words could not express. A new, deeper understanding and acceptance of one another hovered over everyone in the room that night. Hugs and tears said what words could not.

Later that night, we walked Dad and "Mumsy" outside to their car and said our goodbyes. We watched their black BMW drive out of our neighborhood, and I wondered what their conversation would be on the way home and how they would process all the introductions and personalities of the evening.

What did they really think of meeting, not just a long-lost daughter, but an entire family: son-in-law, granddaughters, grandsons-in-law, and great-grandchildren? What would they think of our personalities, temperaments, lifestyle, faith, home? Was it too much too soon?

The emotions had started to thaw and catch up in time with the forgiveness that was given in our first phone conversation.

But where would it go from here?

Tom: Honesty

Memories are fragile things.
What Tanya and I each remember about our lives together and apart is drawn from fragments of conversations, accounts from others, incomplete journals, and our common and candid search for the truth.

While our memories may differ, the truth and courage we've each needed on our journey are shared challenges.

I now look ahead and consider how my daughter and I can build a future that heals.

While reading Tanya's chapters in this book, I've been given a glimpse of her life of separation, abandonment, loss, and years of life experiences I can never share with her.

Tanya and I have both shared aspects of our story in individual online postings as we wrote this book. We have heard from so many others who have made us aware that we're not alone in our search for reconciliation and forgiveness; our experience has been unique but not uncommon.

I've come to personally believe that any process of reconnection begins with a search for forgiveness, and requires communication, and, above all, honesty. Our story has been an ongoing and highly personal process of forgiveness, which we now share so it may light the way for others to find their own paths to forgiveness.

Tanya and I continue to build on what we have learned. We communicate via e-mail, phone calls, and continue writing and sharing our stories.

Karen and I visited Tanya and our new family several times after our first Christmas reunion. One of those visits gave me the inspiration to write a story that begins on a bridge that we visited with Tanya and Ron.

Many years ago, I drew a sketch while standing on this same arched, concrete-tussled bridge that crosses the Rogue River. My eyes fell on the water some seventy feet below where two rubber rafts floated in the distance.

Sixteen years earlier, I'd taken my third wife Trudi and our two boys on a whitewater rafting adventure that passed under this bridge. I drew a sketch of the river the day that trip ended.

On this second trip to the bridge, I searched my phone and found that sketch in my stored images. Looking at that picture, my mind went to the feelings I experienced when I realized Tanya had forgiven me. And then I silently wondered if someday my sons would ever be able to forgive me so that we too might be reunited.

"What are you thinking?" Tanya stood at my side, looking at me with her searching blue eyes. She was full of unanswered questions for a father she wanted to know.

I searched for an answer. It had been sixteen years since my last visit to this bridge. Not very long compared to the thirty-three years Tanya and I lost. I missed her childhood, her birthdays, her wedding and the birth of my grandchildren. I never saw the pain and loneliness my abandonment caused. I was not there as she matured into a loving wife and mother, a woman of strong faith, a woman with wisdom beyond her years.

How could I have answered her question? Should I have said, "I'm thinking of my sons?" No, I couldn't do that, not that day. We were there sharing a moment on our own personal journey to reconnect. I showed Tanya the sketch on my phone and said, "This place has dramatically changed. When I was here in 1996, you and I were worlds apart."

Ron and Karen joined us on the bridge and I showed them the sketch. I said "I wish I could find the spot where I drew this."

Tanya and I crossed the bridge together as Karen quickly found the spot where the sketch was originally drawn. The four of us took photos and selfies to document the location in a new time. Tanya didn't know how much her love and forgiveness meant at that moment. I could see the past, the present and a hopeful future in my sketch and in the new photograph.

As a bridge connects two distant shores, it provides passage and a means of communication across cold waters. The bridge we stood on—the bridge I had so carefully rendered in pen and ink years before—now served to connect Tanya and Ron to Karen and me.

Tanya and I crossed that bridge together.

Ron, Tom, Karen, Tanya

• • • •

The following day, the four of us traveled to Ashland, Oregon, a picturesque city known for its annual Shakespeare festival.

While there, Tanya and Ron invited us to join them at a Sunday service in nearby Jacksonville, on the way back to their home in Roseburg.

The service was conducted in an outdoor amphitheater, and Karen was eager to hear an inspiring sermon under a clear, sunny sky. Her enthusiasm was shared by Ron and Tanya, who brought their deep Christian faith along for the occasion.

I was happy to be part of this outing, but I'll admit my faith in organized religion is, shall we say, "tempered." I personally believe that if faith comforts and inspires you, you have every right to believe as you choose. While I neither judge those who believe nor believe myself, I'm eternally thankful that faith and the power of forgiveness have played such a big part in allowing me to reconnect with my daughter.

As it happened on this Sunday morning, the notion of "connection" was the theme of the sermon delivered by Pastor Jon Courson at his Applegate outdoor sanctuary.

On the slopes of the grassy amphitheater, as I listened to the pastor's powerful words, I glanced once again into the eyes of my daughter. Then my gaze turned from Tanya to the little girl seated beside me. Her father had offered to share the blanket he had spread on the damp terrace with me. I accepted his invitation and sat on the edge of the blanket. I was instantly caught in his little girl's stare. How can I explain what I saw in that little girl's eyes? There was a reflection, a glimpse, of my own little girl whose childhood I had thrown away and lost forever. I felt happy and sad at the same time. Sad for the lost years with Tanya, yet happy we were together again on that grassy slope.

In the car headed back to Roseburg, I told my story of the little girl seated next to me on the grassy slope. Tanya saw tears well in my eyes as I tried to describe what I felt.

At Ron and Tanya's house, we said our goodbyes and then left for the airport. While on the plane flying south to Santa Barbara, I couldn't shake the image of the little girl seated next to me on the grassy knoll. I longed to share my feelings about that day with Tanya.

The only way I could do that was in a story.

• • • •

An Angel's Gift

In a grass-terraced amphitheater midway up the west slope, the morning's glow filters through trees scattered among seated worshipers. The sun washes a golden glow over faces young and old. A breeze brushes leaves. Emotions are caught by ripples of sunlight floating over a congregation in the Applegate outdoor sanctuary.

All hear powerful words of faith resonating from the raised floor of the theater. The podium cut in sandstone is softened by bright flora of red and green. A pool resonates in a gentle soft

154

sound as a waterfall spills. The power of Jon Courson's voice began to fade as an Angel's stare captures me.

A little girl wrapped in her father's arms peers over his shoulder and softly whispers a question, "Why did you let him sit on our blanket, Daddy?"

Dad simply replies, "He needed a seat off the grass; we should share." The child's father had extended a welcome of fellowship by offering me a place to rest. I sat on the edge of his family's blanket, for comfort and protection from the damp grass of the terrace.

I'm captivated as the angelic child cuddles and sways to hymns played by the strings of a single guitar.   I'm drawn to the gentle touch of her intertwined fingers woven tightly to her protector. I find myself looking into the past and see what I've missed. I steal a glimpse of my daughter, a grown woman. It's her childhood I lost.

Jon Courson's words ring out a request, "Honor the children assembled here. Gently touch a child near you as we pray for them."

I'm drawn to the dark round eyes of the little girl in her father's arms. I reach over and touch her arm. She clings tightly to her dad and rests her head securely on his shoulder. That face, painted with heavenly eyes, looks deep into my soul.

Instantly overwhelmed, an unexpected joy fills my heart. I feel the Angel tilt her head, her skin as soft as a rose petal rests on my hand.

The gift of an Angel offers me a glimpse of the past.

• • • •

Not long after our visit to Ashland and Roseburg, an email arrived in my Outlook. A difficult and intimate question popped up on my screen: "What made you change the way you've conducted your life?"

Tanya's question was no longer one posed between strangers. This question was from my daughter and deserved a response. I was apprehensive as I considered the honesty her question demanded.

Will Tanya understand, will I lose her again when she truly understands the suffering and pain I've caused others in my life? If I were to paint a response how would it look? Would it be abstract, complex, visually indecipherable like a Jackson Pollack canvas? Or will it be more like a Norman Rockwell, pristine, precise, and clear? I want it to be an accurate picture, an illustration of myself as a past liar—the embodiment of my Demon—now in hues of change.

Tanya's quiet reserve guards a temperament of inner strength, emotion, and faith. Holding things inside is one of many characteristics we share. Intimacy requires truth, commitment and understanding. Feelings of abandonment do not encourage intimacy.

Tanya's struggle with loss forced her forward and onto a path to adulthood early in life. Now as the wife of a Baptist minister, she counsels young couples on marriage, works with those contemplating divorce, and provides insights on faith to women. She sees life from birth to death. She has found faith, and through her life experiences has built the commitment and honesty required for true intimacy.

It has taken a long time for me to deal with a sense of childhood neglect and to find genuine intimacy. My path to understanding came through a classic recommendation in counseling: "Write a letter to those you have hurt. You don't have to send it, just write it."

My letter became a chapter, then two, and finally ended as I identified the Demon that fed on patterns of destructive behaviors that had followed me out of the tenements of Hoboken and into my adult life. As I searched for answers and fought to rid myself of the Demon, I found a path that would lead to change.

The examination of one failed relationship after another forced me to ask "Why?" The "Why" became clear as I stripped away the layers of crusted paint from the canvas of my life. I peeled back yellowing and cracked pigments and found years of insecurity. To restore and build an honest image, new brush strokes now needed to be applied by my hand, directed by those who touched my life, with details added by an unseen master.

156

As I reread page after page of my own words, I see a person I no longer recognize, a person who was plagued by the Demon I despise. It's like a reformed smoker who now can't stand the smell of cigarettes. The non-smoker looks in disgust at the inconsiderate smoke blown into the air to be inhaled by others. It's the same for a reformed liar, now more judgmental of the slightest little omission or deception.

Like a recovering addict, I recognize and accept my addiction, the most fundamental requirement for overcoming it. I look the Demon in the eye and see him for what he is: a liar, not to be toyed with, never to be trusted.

The Demon can be vanquished and ultimately defeated, but it takes a formidable, heat-tempered weapon. That weapon is Honesty.

I've exposed the canvas of my life, a life filled with pain and lies.

I've sought forgiveness, and as a master paints over old canvases to change and create new works of art, I will be changed. I shall never forget the buried images of an abandoned little girl or of a family torn apart.

Today, my self-portrait begins with the truth, a truth that had brought me back to my daughter, a daughter who has given me the greatest gift of all: forgiveness.

The answer to Tanya's question "What made you change the conduct of your life?" is a simple one. Honesty.

Tom G. Carey & Tanya Laeger

Tanya: Ultimately

From the surprise of "the call" and hearing my father's voice for the first time in three decades, to my father's discovery of grandchildren and great grandchildren previously unknown to him, this has been quite an experience.

The joys and complexities of merging two families' lives have been profound. Ours is a happy-ending story. Many, if not most, attempted family reconnections do not end on such a positive note.

Surviving the rejection and hurt I experienced following "the lunch" at age sixteen, I was apprehensive when it was my husband Ron's turn to consider finding his birth mother. I didn't want him to suffer the hurt and rejection I had.

Ron was adopted when just ten days old. As was common in that era, his adoptive parents chose not to tell him, or his sister, they had been adopted. As with most family secrets, his adoption came to light at a most inconvenient time, during our pre-marriage counseling.

A co-worker of mine at the time, and a friend of Ron's family mentioned that Ron and his sister were both adopted. I was bewildered and wondered why he had never mentioned it to me in our nearly two years of dating. I gingerly brought up the subject and asked if it was possible that he could be adopted. He looked at me like I was crazy.

Ron immediately went to inquire of his brother, who was twenty years his senior, about whether or not he was adopted. His brother confirmed the adoption with no further comment.

Ron was nineteen at the time, and didn't feel the need to look for his birth parents.

It wasn't until he was in his forties that his curiosity and desire to get his backstory surfaced. Ron's adoptive parents had both passed away, so he hired a Confidential Intermediary to help locate his birth mother. The CI soon located Ron's birth mother and informed her that her son would like to contact her. His mother declined phone contact, but allowed Ron to write a letter and tell her about his life.

The terse response was not what Ron had hoped for: "I'm glad you had a good life, but I prefer we have no further contact."

This is the harsh reality of many attempted reconnections. To see Ron suffer the pain of that rebuff was excruciating. Even though we know people are not always in a place emotionally to revisit a vulnerable time from the past, we feel the pain of rejection and unmet expectations.

How do you know when and how to approach this delicate situation? I thought my father handled it brilliantly when he called Ron and asked if I was in a good place to receive a call from him. Not everyone is. There are often unresolved emotions, or long-held secret shame, or fears buried by years of reimagined history.

This was the case with both my father and my husband's mother. In each scenario, they kept the birth of a child secret from their families. I can't even imagine what carrying a burden like that for decades can do to one's soul.

Because of my more subdued temperament, I approached reconnection with my father with cautious reserve. I didn't want to experience even more pain and was unsure about rekindling this relationship. It had caused such heartache in the past, and I was uncertain I wanted to invite "Rejection: The Sequel," into this season of my life. I'm sure my father was aware of my reserve, as he gave me space for my cautious, but willing, further contact.

Because I'm not the hyper-expressive type, a tempered approach helped me slowly wade into emotional waters of uncertain depth. I was allowed to survey the map of this journey before allowing my heart and emotions to outrun what my mind could reconcile.

I had a sweet mentor from church who shared her wise and insightful counsel, "If you choose to reunite, remember that although you are related by blood, you are in reality strangers meeting for the first time as adults." This helped me to look forward to the "discovery" of a new person rather than trying to make sense out of the past or to answer the "why" questions of a life lived decades ago.

Reframing the situation allowed for a realistic discovery of the man with whom I had reunited, and to understand who he is at this point in his life. Hopefully, we live, learn and grow over the years. Who I *was* isn't always who I *am*.

When evaluating reconnection, it is helpful to consider some of the following questions: What will happen if you don't click with one another or other new "family members?" What if you feel insignificant, inferior, or superior? What if you live worlds apart in faith, status, or economic strata?

Faced with these questions, I encourage others to give themselves time and space to answer them and to consider the potential consequences of those answers.

In reality, we do not know the motivations of the one seeking reconciliation. It takes time to build trust and to bridge the years of estrangement. I encourage anyone in this situation to weigh motives carefully. Decide ahead of time what your motivations are and whether or not the other person is in a place where they can constructively revisit the past.

There is in each of us a yearning to see the face of our biological family and a longing to know where we come from as a way of understanding our heritage. Most families are broken in some areas. Relationships are fragile even in the most "normal" of families. Time is fleeting. The possibilities of reconnecting with a lost parent, child, or sibling are many and varied.

In Ernest Hemingway's famous short story, "The Capitol of the World," he tells of a son who had run off to Madrid, Spain. After years of no contact and coming to a point of desperation, the father travels to Madrid and puts an ad in the local newspaper reading, "Paco, meet me at the Hotel Montana at noon on Tuesday. All is forgiven! Love, Papa." When the father arrived at the square in front of the hotel, eight hundred young men named Paco (common name in Spain) showed up searching for their father's forgiveness.

The power of this story pierces the veil of the heart, acknowledging our longing for forgiveness and acceptance when we know we've blown it and, in all reality, don't deserve to be forgiven.

This is called grace.

The basis of Hemingway's short story is the "Prodigal Son" taken from the Bible. Jesus tells a story of a man with two sons. The younger asks his father to give him his share of his estate, and he took everything he was given, set off for a distant land, and there squandered all his wealth on prostitutes and wild living.

When he had depleted his inheritance and had nothing left, he was driven to work in squalor. He was hungry, cold, and alone. The story relates that it was then that he "came to his senses." He remembered that his father treated his servants better than what he was experiencing and that filled him with humility and he returned home to his father.

To his surprise, the father, who had longingly awaited his son's return, saw him a long way off and, filled with compassion, ran to him and embraced him.

The son discovered that he did not have to "earn" his way back into his father's love. His father's love never left him, as it had always been there awaiting his acceptance of it. It was time to celebrate because the son that was lost had now been found.

In a general sense, I feel this is our story, only turned upside down. It was the father who went away to a distant land to live his own life. When he returned, he received forgiveness and acceptance from the daughter he left behind, who was no longer a little girl, but a grown woman.

Ultimately, this story is about God, the Father, who lovingly, longingly peers down the corridors of time, and awaits his children to "come to their senses" and return home to His loving embrace.

Because I believe in God, this is my model for forgiveness. I have and continue to receive it on a daily basis, so how could I not extend it when the opportunity came for my father to return?

We can all lose our way in life. Sometimes it's a short journey. For others, it can be oceans of separation and decades of time passing before there is an awakening in the spirit, a time of reflection over a life filled with joys and sorrows, victories and regrets.

Yet we will know when the time is right to reach out, to initiate the conversation, and how to be patient while awaiting the outcome.

God has a plan.

Keep an open heart, and soon enough His plan will be shown to you.

§ § § §

Tanya's Testimonial

Delivered on July 31, 2011
Wellspring Bible Fellowship, Roseburg Oregon

Forgiveness: Baggage in the Attic

Warning: This is going to be a PG -13 testimony with some adult themes. If you don't want your wee ones to hear this and you don't want to do a lot of explaining after church, or if you are sensitive to adult subject matter/abuse, it might be a good idea to slip out the room for a bit.

I think my husband asked me to talk about my experience because he knows I have had a long and winding road in my "journey to forgiveness." For me, it wasn't a one time and forget it kind of deal.

Many years ago there was a book called "Doorway to Discipleship" and it basically talked about inviting Jesus into the symbolic rooms of spiritual house. Allowing Jesus to turn on the light, arrange the furniture in family room, where the family relates, in the dining room, where family converses, etc. I really had thought that I had allowed Jesus into every part of my spiritual house, but just like Columbo…"there's just this one little thing." Every once in awhile, something would happen that would trigger anxiety, and fear. That is how the Lord let me know I had some baggage in the attic of my spiritual house. It was safely tucked away in the darkness and dust of the attic, and I only visited it when these uninvited guests would come upon me. Jesus lovingly let me know that we needed to take a trip to the attic together. This time He would turn on the light, and we could go through my baggage together.

My mom got married when she was 17, her senior year in high school. Her new husband had to sign her report cards. After she graduated, he moved her to New York where his family lived. When she got pregnant with me, her best friend, who happened to also be her cousin, came to NY to be with my mom. My dad got her pregnant too…so somewhere in this world I have a half brother who is also a cousin. He was also messing around with his college professor. (Talk about a soap opera). My dad was also very abusive, as well as an avid adulterer. After I was born, he pushed my mom and I down a flight of stairs. Mom finally decided to leave him. One day I was living with a mommy and daddy, the next day I didn't have a daddy anymore.

There would be no birthday cards, no Christmas cards, no calls or contact of any kind. Along with packing my favorite life-sized doll with the pink floppy hat in the suitcase, I also packed with me that day the shoes of abandonment in the suitcase of my mind.

My mom took me back to southern CA., and she married again, and that marriage was annulled. Then she and another man tried to rent the same apartment on the beach in Coronado. She won. But he got the apartment next door. One day she left a paper grocery bag on the stove burner, he found it and saved the day. Apparently, that was enough grounds to get married again. They quickly got married on the Coronado beach, both in shorts, with a justice of the peace, and 2 witnesses, without my mom ever having met my dad's family. Word to the wise girls, please don't do this!! This new dad was in the SEAL team and UDT, charming, but one tough cookie.

Our first trip to see my new family. So excited. Other grandma was super crabby and I was looking forward to getting a new one. My mom bought me a brand new dress and we all went to meet our new family. Drove up and saw a dirty trailer with chickens running in and out. Long table on the outside where they had they put their dirty dishes. Every few days they would hose them down with a garden hose – this is how they washed their dishes. Went in to meet new grandma, sitting on couch looking at me from head to toe, and said "this is not my real granddaughter." Into the suitcase of my mind, I neatly folded my new little dress of rejection and being unwanted in my new little family.

After some adult talk, my new grandpa asked me if I wanted to watch a movie. It started out with a cartoon version of Snow White and the Seven Dwarfs, it soon morphed into a porn movie, I was 5... – Mom scooped me up and carried me to back bedroom – dark, smelly, scary, gross brown stained teeth in a dirty glass on the counter. She left me alone in the room. When I was trying to think of a way to describe how I felt, a theme song popped in my mind. I normally don't think in songs, and when you hear it, you'll be glad I don't...

They're creepy and they're kooky,
Mysterious and spooky,
They're altogether ooky,
My step-dad's family.

I couldn't wait to leave that place and go home, taking with me in the suitcase of my mind, the carefully folded garment of feeling that there we're creepy, spooky things in the world. I didn't have the words for it at the time, but it was my first realization of the presence of evil.

Years later, when I was in Junior High, we visited crabby grandma and grandpa in CA. All the extended family got together to watch those old family movies on the reel to reel, picture of mom sitting on lap of some guy (blue jeans, white t-shirt, with pack of cigarettes rolled up in the sleeve of his t-shirt), asked,. "who is that." Crabby grandma said a few colorful words and walked out of the room, and after an awkward silence mom said...that's your real dad. (it was the first time I had seen a picture of him since he had left when I was 3). That night she asked if I wanted to meet him. He apparently had moved to nearby Santa Barbara. I was mostly curious as to what he looked like.

She made arrangements to meet at a restaurant on the marina. They ordered me a salad that came in the shape of a swan. Couldn't eat it because I was overwhelmed with emotion and just cried the entire time. He asked if I had any questions. I just asked if he had a new family and he said he had a wife named Bunny but no kids. He also said she didn't know about us. He asked me if I wanted to see the buildings he had designed (architect) so he took me for a short drive and when he dropped me off, he asked if I would write him. I was thrilled. I couldn't wait to start getting to know this man who I actually looked a lot alike. Got home and was so excited and wrote my very first letter

165

about my life, and school, and included a picture of me in a cute little cheer leading pose with pom-poms and everything. I was so excited to mail my first letter to his office address. A few days later, the letter was returned unopened. We sent it again, same thing. Finally, my mom sent it "receipt requested" and when it was returned it had my dad's signature with the words (recipient does not accept). I knew enough to know that it wasn't just the letter that wasn't being accepted, it was me. Into the suitcase, I carefully folded the garment of rejection, and again feeling unwanted and unloved. This was getting to be a familiar theme in the suitcase of my mind.

I never really felt a part of our home. I constantly fought the distinct feeling that I was the old, ugly discarded wrapping paper that came along with the package (my mom was the prize). I always felt on edge and on alert when I was at home.

We lived in a sexually charged house; porn magazines came every month in that brown paper cover. We lived in an average house for the time, 5 people, one bath. The bathroom didn't have a lock on it. But right inside there was a drawer you could pull out and it would block the door from opening all the way. My dad would always threw a fit, along with a slew of colorful language about my blocking the door in the bathroom. He never shut the door. For some reason, even though I was a super compliant kid, I kept doing it even though it made him mad.

Finally, one day I was in the bathroom taking a bath when my dad came home. For some reason, no one else was in the house. Dad tried to get into the bathroom, but thankfully I had the door blocked. After a few choice words he left for a minute and I was relieved. Then he came back with a kitchen knife. He started to jimmy the drawer closed through the opening. I was literally paralyzed with fear, I was screaming on the inside but no sound came out. I knew that this was not going to end well. I was right. That day I learned that the world is indeed unsafe. The people that are suppose to protect you, don't. Into the suitcase, I placed carefully folded undergarments of shame, guilt, embarrassment and powerlessness.

166

Along with the abuse, came its twin, "the threat." My threat was that if you tell anyone, you will destroy our family. Well, I loved my mom and my brother and sister and certainly didn't want to be the one to destroy the family. So into the suitcase, went in the **weight of responsibility** of keeping the dark, family secret. Remember, we were the house next door. The normal, average American family, except that once when I got home from school, he had a rape kit out on the glass dining room table. He was a sheriff's deputy. He was arresting people for the very thing he was doing; but somehow there was a disconnect.

My mom was always trying to get me to have a better relationship with my dad, to spend more time with him. One day he took a friend of mine (his best friends daughter) out for "bonding" time. He took us to the woods, told me to stay in the truck, and he took my little friend to the woods. I learned that day that I was helpless to protect others. Into the suitcase went the hoodie of powerlessness and shame. I knew she was being violated and there was nothing I could do but wait until it was all over. They both came out of the woods, dad got on the drivers side of the truck, I was in the middle, and my friend got in next to me. Everyone stared straight out the truck window and not a single word was spoken all the way home. My life as a secret agent continued.

My dad was formidable and you didn't mess with him. I remember him telling me once about the anatomy of the body parts of the men and women he had killed when he was in the SEALs, he kept them as a souvenirs.

A year or two later, we were at school, watching a film in PE class that talked about abuse and that if you are carrying a secret, you need to tell someone. I churned inside for days, not knowing what to do. I finally decided to tell my mom. What a relief to finally share the dark secret. Her first response was disbelief. But my dad finally came into the my bedroom where it had happened, and confessed. My dad was in the Seal teams, a tough, harsh man. It was the first, and last time, I ever saw him cry. He told my mom he would never do it again and I felt such a great relief. Until about ½ an hour later, we had both walked outside and in the driveway he turned and looked at me and said, well, if you ever need $20 bucks, you know where to come and what to do to get it. I was devastated. The fear would continue. Into my suitcase I put my value of $20 bucks, and even then I felt a little insulted because I was pretty sure that was on the low end of the pay scale. I immediately got a job so I would never have to ask for money and could buy my own school clothes. I also packed into my now overstuffed suitcase, the coat of distrust. Emotional apologies weren't to be trusted, and neither were the people who gave them. Fear and trepidation would remain my constant companion, although nothing major ever happened after that.

16th birthday my mom gave me a big, green book called the "Living Bible." I thought it was a kind of weird thing to give a girl for her birthday. But I remember going into my room, where I spent most of my time, and starting reading at page 1 (where else would you start to read a book?) I got through most of Genesis and remember thinking, "wow, this is really well written." I didn't know it was talking about real places or people, I actually thought it was fiction. But just in case, I remember saying, "God if you are out there and are real, would you please love me?"

The answer came about 6 months later all wrapped up in a Centralia Tiger's baseball uniform with the number 16 on it. Had I only known that my savior was going to look that good in a baseball uniform, I might have come around sooner. #16, Ron Laeger and I started dating and taking me to church. Frankly, it was a very odd experience for me. I had never seen a bunch of grown-ups all dressed up singing the same songs I had never heard of. But we kept dating and he kept taking me to church and after awhile I got the hang of it and the routines became more comfortable.

We got married a month after I graduated, thinking that my knight in shining armor was going to take me to his castle, and the suitcase would finally disappear. Instead I carried my suitcase with me into my new marriage. After about 3 months of being married, and Ron now pursuing other things (work, college, building a house), I started trying on those old, comfortable clothes in that old suitcase. Ron didn't understand it. And so, out of desperation I knelt down on our green shag rug, and asked The Lord into my life. But even that didn't make the suitcase disappear. I started reading my bible, we started our little family and eventually my suitcase got shoved in the closet for the most part. Busyness, kids and daily life was mode of the day.

When reading the bible one day, it talked about "honoring your father and mother." I thought surely that didn't apply to me. And then I sensed the Voice I would come to love to hear – that still, quiet whisper that said…"not so fast, sister." I thought how could God possibly ask me to honor someone that was so dishonorable and had violated my trust? I battled it in my mind that God would surely not expect me to apply this particular passage to my life. But He didn't relent. So I started thinking about how I could honor him authentically without ignoring the truth of the past. I came to separate the "position" the Lord had given him in my life for provision. He had a hard work ethic; I could honestly be thankful that I always had food and a shelter. God provided that provision through him. It was the best I could do at the time.

Several years later, I was watching the news and it had a story about a guy who was going to prison for molesting a girl. I was in my 30's, and I never knew that what had happened to me was illegal. I knew it was wrong, but I didn't know someone could go to prison for it. I tucked it away in my suitcase. And a few months later, my dad came to our door. It was weird because he never came to see me after I was married. He had come to ask forgiveness for what he had done. I never felt I held a grudge or resentment. I really didn't feel anything at all, and I didn't know what to do. I said I forgave him. I felt better but it didn't make the suitcase disappear. I put it up in the attic for safe keeping.

Then one day, years later, my dad called out of the blue. He and my mom had divorced, so it was a little weird that he was calling me. He had just gotten married to a girl my age a couple weeks before. He said, I have some news…my first thought was, oh know they are going to have a baby. That's going to be weird. Then he told me that he was going to have heart surgery, a 4-way bypass. Which was strange because he was still running 5 miles and was in great health, but I think for the first time in his life, he was scared. A couple of nights after his surgery, we heard knocking on our door about 3 in the morning. A man who had known my dad, said, "Tanya, I'm sorry to tell you that your dad is dead." He's in the ER at the hospital. He was 50. So Ron asked me if I wanted to go and see him. I said, "why?" Well honey, sometimes it's good to say goodbye and have some closure. None of my other family could be reached at the time.

So, we walked into the ER, and there lay my dad, the man that I had feared my entire life, laying on a gurney, naked with a blue paper drape laid over him, and a toe tag hanging off his big toe. This man who had been bigger than life, life lifeless on a stainless steel table. In some part of me there was a sense of relief, but it was also mixed with a strange concoction of competing emotions; sadness for what never was, but could have been, grief, relief, sadness for my brother and sister.

My hope and prayer is that in God's amazing grace, He gave my dad time to make things right before He was ushered to his eternal destiny. He had his own suitcase. But his dying didn't make my suitcase disappear.

My life went on but every once in awhile something would trigger in my spirit, like an uninvited guest, and I would want to go and rummage through the suitcase to see if the clothes still fit – they always did. I was trying to find a way I could forgive authentically without dismissing the reality of what had occurred. It was when I truly connected with what Jesus said on the cross, "Father forgive them for they don't know what they do." So I applied that to my situation...Father forgive my dad, he had no idea that a few moments of self- gratification would cause lifelong imprints of insecurity and feelings of having no value. That a few moments would affect my future husband for years to come because I had a warped view of sexuality. That it would affect how I relate to men in general. I applied the same principle to my biological dad. Father forgive my dad, for he had no idea that abandoning and rejecting his daughter would have lingering effects of insecurity and internal battles of not being wanted or loved.

How do I know for sure that I have forgiven them...because it is one of my heart's great desires to have my dad greet me at the gates of heaven. I pray for my biological dad and his family also that they would come to know and receive this incredible gift that God has so generously bestowed on me. His new family doesn't know about us. He's carrying a lot of baggage in his own suitcase of life.

I've come to the conclusion that Forgiveness is not making the suitcase disappear, it is keeping the light on in the attic. Jesus is the light. Shining the light of God's truth to see the realities of life and put the times of "great sadness" in proper perspective. Ps. 139 says There is no darkness with God, darkness is like daylight to Him. I always picture God as having the first night vision goggles. He shines His radiant light into our dark attics. He wipes away the dust of old memories, and the cobwebs of fear and insecurity. Occasionally He still accompanies me to the attic to sort through the old clothes, put them in proper perspective, but now He always leaves the light on. Kind of like the hotel commercial.

Sometimes when Jesus and I come down out of the attic, I imagine us sitting and sharing some conversation and chai tea. Occasionally there is a knock on the door. I open it to find someone standing there clutching their own suitcase. And we invite them in and Jesus helps them sort through their own times of great sadness. And then we close the suitcase, put it back in the attic. And we know that Jesus always leaves the light on.

For God has not given us a spirit of fear,
but of power and of love and of a sound mind.
(2Ti 1:7 NKJ)

· · · · · · · · ·

171

Tom G. Carey & Tanya Laeger

Epilogue

Tom: 2021 Update

Tanya and I have continued to build our relationship. It has been expanded with visits, emails, and phone calls, and includes getting to know my granddaughters and eight great-grandchildren. We are building our own traditions as a family and our visits become more joyous each time we get to gather.

As a child I remember Thanksgivings at my Grandparents. All the cousins, aunts, and uncles bustling around as my grandmother worked in the kitchen. Children would be playing while aunts and uncles would be consumed in exuberant conversations. The noise levels reached a crescendo when my grandmother announced it was time to sit. There was always a separate table for the children with all the giggles, smiles and excitement of looking for the wish bone.

The memories of those Thanksgiving dinners always warmed my heart. For several years now, Karen and I have joined Tanya and our extended family for Thanksgiving. I am now sitting at the adult table but the joy I feel as I sit and watch the children at their table is indescribable. New memories blend with the old as the years go by. This is family. The letters addressed to me as Dear Great Grandpa Tom are more precious than any material possessions.

I am so proud of Tanya and Ron for taking the message we expressed in this book on the road. Not everyone will be in a place to forgive or offer forgiveness but if just one person gets to experience what we have shared, all our work will have meaning.

It has taken a long time, but the best is yet to come. Tanya, I love you and I'm so proud of you.

-- Dad

Tanya: 2021 Update

. . . and our amazing story continues to unfold day by extraordinary day. So much has evolved since the time my dad and I collaborated in writing our story almost 10 years ago. I relish how our relationship continues to emerge into something beyond what I could have ever hoped for or imagined. The love my dad and his wife, Karen, have lavished not only on me, but on our entire extended family has been unfathomable. My heart overflows with new-found joy and gratitude every time I hear their voices say "grandpa or great grandpa Tom." To see Dad and Karen sitting around our Thanksgiving table in animated conversation with friends and family is not only something I never could have imagined 10 years ago, it brings with it a soul healing I didn't know was possible .

We are living proof that it is never too late to take the next step to restore a broken (or non-existent) relationship.

"What would it be like to travel the country?" was my husband's probing question on a long overdue date night in September of 2020. "I know you finished writing the book but I don't think the book is done with you." We dreamed out loud and percolated the idea of traveling the country, sharing our story and using the book as an icebreaker for other people to share their forgiveness stories to record for a YouTube channel. We'd call it . . . *Forgiveness Road.*

This queen of homebodies who gets my security from home, routine and the status quo bought an RV (we don't camp), sold our *beloved* home in the Pacific Northwest, quit our jobs and set out on the adventure of a lifetime. Being out of my comfort zone is an understatement. But I'm learning that every time I step out into the unfamiliar, I step into an unknowable future rife with excitement and adventure. Courage is being built one baby step at a time.

And so the story continues, although we don't know where this adventure will lead . . . or where we will end up living after this excursion – (yes, I'm already dreaming of decorating my someday, somewhere house.)

This one thing I know–I will forever have the love of my father that now enables me to view life from different lenses–to dare to dream–to dare to explore–to dare to step out into an unknown, adventurous future.

I hope you'll reach out to us on our journey to share your stories of forgiveness and let us know how YOU are navigating your own path to forgiveness. You can always reach me directly at forgivenessroad@gmail.com. I look forward to hearing from you and be sure to stay in touch on our *Forgiveness Road* YouTube Channel, Website, Facebook or Instagram!

Join the journey . . .

~Tanya

Back row LtoR: Grandpa Tom Carey, Ron Laeger, Lindsi Holland, Josh Holland, Sawyer Holland, Misti Poe, Chris Poe, Lucy Poe, Mumsy Karen Carey
Front row LtoR: Lillian Holland, Clara Holland, Maddie Dailey, Kali Dailey, Jim Dailey, Tanya Laeger, Abigail Holland, Judah Holland

The great-grandkids. LtoR: Sawyer Holland, Abigail Holland,
Clara Holland, Lillian Holland, Maddie Dailey, Judah Holland

About the Authors

Tom G. Carey has lived in Santa Barbara for more than 50 years as a respected architect, real estate developer, and artist. He has contributed numerous articles to multiple travel magazines, and has authored the books *Sketches of a Good Life* and *Away We Go Italy*. Tom and his wife Karen are active in the local arts community and when not traveling, enjoy golf and painting.

Tanya and her husband Ron are currently traveling the country in search of remarkable forgiveness stories for their YouTube channel, **Forgiveness Road.** Experiencing life transformation because of her own story, her desire is to share, not only her story, but *yours*. If you have a story that might bring encouragement, inspiration, and hope to others, she'd love to hear from you. She hopes you'll reach out to her and Ron on their journey and share your stories of forgiveness and of how YOU are navigating your own path to forgiveness. Because wherever there is forgiveness, there is a profound story yet untold. You can always reach Tanya directly at forgivenessroad@gmail.com. Ron and Tanya are available for speaking engagements, conferences and media opportunities as they travel the Forgiveness Road together with you!

Tom G. Carey & Tanya Laeger